RAISING YOUR SON WITH INTENTION

Fostering Emotional Resilience

MYRON WINGEN

Dedication

To young men who aren't scared to embrace their emotions, bravely navigate their inner world of feelings, ignore outdated notions of how they're supposed to behave, and embrace every aspect of their humanity with open arms.

Here's to parents who have their sons' backs, who listen with intent and support them with all their hearts, who challenge the 'boys will be boys' cliché and root for their sons to understand and control their emotions, setting them on a path to become emotionally intelligent and compassionate men.

And here's to the world that's coming for them, a place where being open-hearted is seen as a form of courage, where caring for others is a form of clout, and where being authentic is the golden ticket to realizing their most remarkable abilities.

May this book shine like a lighthouse, offer wisdom, and prove what mindful parenting can achieve. May it light the way for a new wave of young men to flourish, honor their feelings, and help build a future where tenderness and togetherness win the day.

Acknowledgement

This book wouldn't have come to life without the wonderful people who have inspired and supported its creation.

My deepest gratitude goes to the boys and young men who have opened up about their experiences, shedding light on the journey to emotional fortitude.

A shout-out to the moms and dads who have wholeheartedly adopted mindful parenting; your dedication to your sons is a constant source of inspiration.

I am also grateful for the researchers, educators, and therapists whose work has informed this book. Big thanks to my colleagues and mentors for their guidance and support and my family and friends for believing in me.

May this book serve as a resource and inspiration for raising emotionally intelligent boys who thrive.

Why This Book?

This guide was crafted for parents eager to raise emotionally intelligent, resilient boys but who feel a bit lost when it comes to dealing with their boys' deep feelings. It's for those who reject the outdated norms of masculinity and want to empower their sons to express their emotions fully.

Within these pages, you'll find Hands-on tips, insightful guidance, and transformative exercises to help your son:

- **Understand and manage his emotions:** He'll know how to recognize and channel his emotions, from irritation and worry to sorrow and happiness, in good ways.

- **Develop resilience:** He'll learn to recover from setbacks, take on challenges, and approach life's unknowns with a can-do attitude.

- **Sharpening his ability to care for others:** He'll learn to tune into other people's emotions, which will lead to more kindness and stronger bonds.

- **Turn into a young man who's both respectful and responsible:** He'll develop a strong sense of self, figure out how to set healthy boundaries and be accountable for his actions.

To sum up, this book aims to equip you with the tools and insights to raise a son who not only thrives in the world but also contributes to it with kindness, empathy, and emotional intelligence.

Table of Contents

Introduction

Our boys encounter challenges from the get-go. Society bombards them with notions about what it takes to be a "true man," creating a strict, often unspoken "boy code" that dictates their behavior, thoughts, and feelings.

Phrases like **"Boys don't cry," "Man up,"** and **"Don't be a sissy,"** frequently heard on playgrounds and in homes, slowly erode a boy's right to be emotionally open. They tell him that being vulnerable is a sign of weakness, that it's shameful to be sensitive, and that showing emotions should be avoided.

Picture a young boy, his face flushed with frustration, tears welling in his eyes after losing a game. He wants to express his feelings and be comforted, but the boy code whispers in his ear, "Don't cry, or you'll look weak." So, he holds back his tears, tightens his fists, and retreats into silence.

This is the reality for many boys today. They grow up in a world that often discourages them from expressing their emotions. They're taught to suppress their feelings, hide their vulnerabilities, and put on a brave face.

This suppression of emotions can lead to severe issues. Boys who are unable to express their feelings in healthy ways may face trouble with anger, anxiety, depression, and forming deep connections. They might resort to aggression, substance misuse, or isolation as coping mechanisms.

The boy code limits boys' emotional expression and restricts their ability to develop empathy and compassion. When boys are taught to suppress their emotions, they often struggle to relate to and understand others' emotions, making it difficult for them to have healthy relationships, navigate social situations, and resolve conflicts peacefully.

Moreover, the boy code reinforces harmful stereotypes about masculinity, promoting the idea that men must be tough, controlling, and emotionally detached. This limited view of manhood can restrict boys' potential and prevent them from being their authentic selves.

But there's hope. As parents, educators, and caregivers, we can change the boy code and create a new way of raising boys that values emotional intelligence, vulnerability, and authentic expression. This is where intentional parenting comes in.

Intentional parenting means being actively engaged and responsive to our kids' needs. It's about fostering an environment where they feel safe sharing their emotions, exploring who they are, and reaching their full potential.

When we parent with intention, we defy the restrictive norms of the boy code and create space for boys to be themselves. We teach them that it's okay to feel a wide range of emotions, from joy and excitement to sadness and fear. We help them handle their feelings effectively, communicate their needs clearly, and build healthy relationships.

Intentional parenting is not about being perfect or having all the answers. It's about being there for our kids with love, empathy, and a readiness to learn and grow with them. It's about creating a supportive space where they're seen, heard, and valued for being authentic.

This book, **"Raising Your Son with Intention: Fostering Emotional Resilience,"** is a guide for parents who want to raise boys who are not just solid and capable but also emotionally aware, resilient, and kind. **It provides actionable advice and insights to help you:**

- **Understand the inner world of boys:** Comprehend the unique challenges and pressures boys face today.

- **Establish a strong bond:** Build a trusting, empathetic, and communicative parent-child relationship.

- **Handle challenging emotions:** Teach your son to manage anger, worries, and sadness.

- **Promote self-awareness and emotional literacy:** Help your son recognize, comprehend, and healthily express his emotions.

- **Encourage empathy and compassion:** Motivate your son to empathize with others and form strong, meaningful bonds.

- **Develop resilience:** Help your son build the strength to tackle obstacles, recover from disappointments, and prosper despite difficulties.

Raising emotionally resilient boys is an active process. It requires deliberate effort, mindful presence, and a readiness to question old-fashioned norms. It's about shaping a world where boys feel free to express their emotions and grow into well-rounded men.

This book is an invitation to join the intentional parenting journey. It's a call to action to raise a generation of boys who are strong on the outside and inside—boys ready to handle life's complexities with bravery, empathy, and emotional strength.

In the following chapters, we will explore boys' specific challenges, outline the core principles of intentional parenting, and give you practical tools to help your son develop emotional resilience. It's time to rewrite the boy code and establish a new vision for raising thriving boys.

Chapter 1: Understanding the Inner World of Boys

"The strongest people aren't always the people who win, but the people who don't give up when they lose." - Ashley Hodgeson

This quote tells us a lot about the strength we want to build in our boys – it's not just about being physically strong or showing off who's boss. It's a strength that resides deep within, an emotional resilience that allows them to face challenges, setbacks, and even failures with courage and determination. But, to understand how to foster this inner strength, we must first understand the complex inner world of boys.

From a young age, boys are tangled in a silent set of expectations and social pressures that mold their feelings. These unwritten "codes" of masculinity can be very powerful, influencing how they perceive themselves, interact with others, and let their emotions out.

One of the most common aspects of this "boy code" is the suppression of emotions. Boys are often taught directly and indirectly that expressing vulnerability is a sign of weakness. They learn to stifle their tears, hide their fears, and slap on a tough-guy act. They're told, "Big boys don't cry," so they learn to bury their emotions deep inside.

This suppression of emotions can twist things up.

When boys can't let their feelings out healthily, those emotions don't just vanish; they often pop up in less desirable ways. Take anger, for example—it becomes an outlet for unexpressed sadness, fear, or frustration. A boy who has been taught to suppress his tears may lash out in anger when he feels hurt or overwhelmed.

This whole boy code thing also affects how boys talk about stuff. Boys might find it difficult to express their needs and emotions, which can lead to misunderstandings, frustration, and strained relationships. They may resort to withdrawing, acting out, or using humor to deflect from difficult conversations. Trouble with talking things through can make it extra hard for them to reach out for help when they're in a rough patch, leaving them feeling even more alone and exacerbating their emotional burdens.

Under this kind of pressure, boys often develop unhealthy coping mechanisms. They may turn to video games, social media, or other forms of escapism to numb their emotions. Some may engage in risky behaviors, seeking thrills and validation to compensate for their feelings of inadequacy. Others may internalize their struggles, leading to anxiety, depression, or even self-harm.

It's crucial to recognize that these "codes" are not baked into boys from the start; they're ideas that society has cooked up and keeps reinforcing. We – that's parents, teachers, and anyone who cares for kids – have got to step up and make room for boys to express how they feel fully.

Understanding the developmental stages of emotional intelligence in boys is crucial in giving them the support they need. Emotional intelligence is not a fixed trait but rather a set of skills that can be learned and nurtured over time. It's about being able to spot, get, handle, and use emotions effectively.

In early childhood, boys mostly try to figure out and name basic emotions like joy, sadness, and anger. They may struggle to differentiate between emotions or understand the nuances of emotional experiences. As they grow, their emotional vocabulary expands, and they get better at naming their feelings and start to see how their thoughts, feelings, and actions all link up.

During adolescence, boys experience hormonal changes and social pressures that can make navigating their emotions even more complex. They may grapple with who they are, how they see themselves, and how they fit in with their pals, all of which can shake up their emotional well-being.

Parents have a super important role in fostering emotional intelligence throughout these growing stages. By creating a safe and supportive environment, we can encourage boys to express their emotions freely without worrying about being judged or ashamed. We can teach them to recognize and name their feelings, figure out what's setting off those feelings, and find good ways to express and manage them.

It's equally important to model emotional intelligence ourselves. When we, as parents, can express our own emotions in healthy ways, we're setting a solid example for our boys to follow. We show them it's totally okay to feel the full range of emotions, from joy and excitement to sadness and disappointment.

Furthermore, we can help boys learn to put

themselves in someone else's shoes by getting them to think about how others feel. We can engage them in conversations about social situations, look at different sides of the story, and encourage them to practice active listening.

Remember, every boy is unique, and his emotional journey will unfold in his own time. There's no magic formula for growing emotionally intelligent sons. What's most important is creating a loving and supportive environment where boys feel free to express how they feel, talk about what they need, and develop the skills they need to thrive.

By understanding boys' inner worlds, questioning restrictive norms, and nurturing their emotional intelligence, we can empower them to break free from the "boy code" shackles and be their genuine selves. We're on track to raise boys who are strong and capable, emotionally resilient, compassionate, and equipped to face the complexities of life with confidence and grace.

Decoding the Boy Code: Unmasking Hidden Emotions

Picture this: A group of boys on the playground. Suddenly, one falls and scrapes his knee, tears welling up. Another boy pats him on the back and tells him, "C'mon, don't act like a little kid; just shake it off!" This moment shines a light on the boy code: big boys don't cry. They're expected to bottle up feelings, especially the "softer" ones like sadness or fear, and put on a brave face.

This code might not be talked about much, but it's got a firm hold on boys. It echoes in gym classes, pops up in movies and video games, and can even be hinted at by adults who mean no harm. It's a message that being open about feelings is not okay and that true masculinity lies in stoicism and strength.

But emotions don't simply vanish when suppressed. They simmer beneath the surface and can pop out when you least expect it. A kid who's been told to "act like a man" can turn his sadness into anger, maybe picking fights or withdrawing into sullen silence. He might struggle to say what he needs, leading to misunderstanding and frustration. Sometimes, he might even start taking risks or using substances to block out those feelings he's not supposed to show.

Decoding the boy code means spotting those hidden feelings. It's about looking beyond the surface behaviors that are pushing them around. It means creating a space where boys feel safe sharing all their feelings—not just the happy or excited ones but also the sadness, fear, and vulnerability.

We're not trying to make boys super sensitive or fragile individuals. We're aiming to let them be themselves, to recognize and deal with their emotions without feeling embarrassed or judged, and to equip them with the tools to handle their emotions with confidence and strength.

We unlock their emotional potential when we help boys decode the boy code. We enable them to talk openly, form solid relationships, and tackle life's ups and downs with courage and compassion. We're building a world where emotional muscle isn't about hiding your soft side but about having the courage to show it.

The Development of Emotional Intelligence in Boys

Think of emotional intelligence as a stronger muscle with practice and guidance. Just as a child's body grows and becomes more capable over time, their ability to understand and handle their feelings evolves, too. This journey of emotional development happens step by step, with each step building upon the last.

In the beginning, a little boy's feelings are straightforward—he's either happy, sad, mad, or scared. If his block tower falls over, he might burst into tears or light up with joy when he sees his favorite toy. These emotions are essential for his learning process. He's starting to figure out his feelings and give names to them, which is like laying down the first layer of understanding his feelings.

As he gets older, he starts to notice that there are different kinds of feelings—like being frustrated isn't quite the same as being angry, or feeling let down is different from feeling sad. He also learns that it's possible to have mixed feelings, like being thrilled and scared about starting school. This deeper understanding helps him make sense of how he reacts and acts.

The next big step is learning to handle those emotions. He discovers that even if he can't always control his feelings, he can choose what he does about them. Maybe he realizes that a deep breath in and out can cool down his anger or that chatting with someone he trusts can ease his worries. Being able to manage his feelings like this is a foundation for bouncing back from tough times with composure.

Parents are like emotional coaches on this journey. When you understand where he's coming from and let him know it's okay to feel that way, you help him trust his emotions. Comforting him when he's having a tough time shows him that feelings aren't something to be scared of or to push away. And when you help him sort out a disagreement, you give him handy skills for dealing with interpersonal challenges.

It's not about getting rid of challenging emotions like anger or sadness. It's about helping him learn to know and be okay with all his feelings, share them well, and learn from them.

This journey of getting to know his emotions isn't a straight line. There will be ups and downs, steps back, and some big feelings. But with your steady support and patient help, you can guide your boy to grow the emotional strength he needs to thrive in a complex world.

Key Points

- **The "Boy Code" Exists:** Societal rules and expectations shape how boys show their feelings and act, often pushing them to hide their emotions. This can make it challenging for boys to talk about their feelings and deal with them healthily.

- **Holding In Emotions Has Consequences:** When boys cannot express their feelings, those feelings don't just vanish. They can manifest in unhealthy ways, such as getting angry quickly, engaging in risky behaviors, or withdrawing from others.

- **Emotional Intelligence Takes Time:** Learning about emotions doesn't happen overnight. It's a process that begins with recognizing simple emotions and grows into a deeper understanding and control. Parents are essential in guiding their kids through this.

- **Every Boy is Unique:** There's no magic formula for every boy's emotional growth. How they develop emotionally depends on their unique personalities, life experiences, and surroundings.

- **Intentional Parenting Makes a Difference:** When parents make an effort to create a safe and supportive environment, they help their sons fully accept their emotions, challenge restrictive norms, and develop the skills they need to thrive.

Self-Reflection Questions

1. How were you taught to express your emotions when you were a kid? Were there emotions you were encouraged or discouraged from sharing? How might those early experiences shape how you raise your child now?

_____

_____

_____

_____

_____

2. How do you react when your son expresses anger or sadness? Are you the type to discourage those emotions, or do you provide a supportive space for him to work through them?

_____

_____

_____

_____

_____

3. What messages are you sending your son about what it means to be a boy and how to handle emotions? Are you perhaps reinforcing outdated stereotypes, or are you challenging those restrictive norms?

_____

_____

_____

_____

_____

4. Do you really understand what your son is going through emotionally? Can you pick up on the little things he doesn't say out loud? Do you truly take

the time to listen and empathize with his experiences?

_____

_____

_____

_____

_____

5. What steps can you take to become more intentional about supporting your son's emotional development? What steps can you take to ensure he feels comfortable and supported in expressing himself fully?

_____

_____

_____

_____

_____

Transformative Exercises

- Create a collection of cards, each featuring a different emotion, such as happiness, sadness, anger, or surprise. Take turns mimicking these feelings and have fun guessing what each other is feeling. This game is an excellent way for boys to become more aware of their own emotions and those of others.

- Encourage your son to keep a journal where he can express his emotions. Whether he writes, draws, or just doodles, it's a personal space where he can express his feelings, enhancing his self-awareness.

- Present your son with imaginary situations involving different emotions (e.g., "What if your friend said something hurtful to you?"). Talk about how he might feel and brainstorm various ways he could react.

- Set aside a particular time to listen to your son. When he talks, repeat what he says in your own words and acknowledge his feelings. This practice strengthens your bond and ensures he feels heard.

- Make it a habit for everyone in the family to share their emotions, maybe during meals or before bed. This practice encourages everyone to communicate openly and shows that sharing feelings is a normal part of family life.

Chapter 2: Building a Foundation of Connection

"Listen earnestly to anything your children want to tell you, no matter what. If you don't listen eagerly to the little stuff when they are little, they won't tell you the big stuff when they are big, because to them all of it has always been big stuff." - Catherine M. Wallace

This quote captures the essence of building a solid connection with your son: giving him your full attention, whether he's talking about something big or small. It's about being there for him, not just physically but emotionally and mentally, in those everyday moments that weave the fabric of your relationship.

Think of a time when someone listened to you. Maybe it was a conversation with a friend, a mentor, or a relative who was all ears, didn't judge, and just got where you were coming from. Recall how it felt to be taken seriously, that warm connection, and knowing someone genuinely cared about your words.

Now, picture giving that same level of attention to your son. Imagine putting everything else on hold, silencing your inner critic, and truly tuning in to his words, emotions, and way of seeing things. This is what intentional parenting is all about—being fully present in the moments you share with your son, fostering a connection that's more than just skin-deep, one that reaches into his innermost thoughts and feelings.

Being present involves more than just sitting in the

same room or doing stuff together. It's about engaging with your son, making eye contact, noticing how he moves and talks, and listening with your entire being. It's about putting your phone away, shutting your computer, and quieting the endless mental checklist that fills our heads.

One of the best ways to build connections is through active listening. It's a kind of listening that's more than just hearing words; it's about getting the feelings, ideas, and needs behind those words. When you listen like this to your son, you're sending a strong message: "You matter. What you think and feel is important. I'm here to listen and understand."

Active listening involves several key components:

- **Paying attention:** Focus only on your son. Look him in the eye, nod, and show interest without saying a word.

- **Reflecting:** Repeat what he tells you to ensure you've got it. "So, you're upset because..."

- **Validating:** Acknowledge and accept his feelings, even if you don't see things the same way. "I can see why that would make you mad."

- **Asking open-ended questions:** Encourage him to open up more. "Tell me more about what happened."

Empathy is another aspect of connection. It's understanding and sharing another person's feelings, stepping into their shoes, and looking at things from their angle. When you respond to your son with empathy, you make a safe space for him to let his guard down and share his feelings without worrying about being judged or feeling ashamed.

Empathetic responses involve:

- **Verbalizing your understanding:** "I can tell you're sad about this."

- **Offering comfort and support:** "It's okay to feel this way. I'm right here with you."

- **Normalizing his feelings:** "Everyone gets frustrated at times. It's normal."

Building a strong parent-child bond requires more than occasional moments of presence and empathy. It's about cultivating an ongoing relationship based on trust, respect, and getting along with each other.

Here are some ways to deepen this connection:

- **Prioritize quality time:** Set aside dedicated time for activities you enjoy, whether playing games, reading, or talking.

- **Show affection:** Let your son know how much you care with hugs, kind words, and little acts of kindness

- **Be a safe space:** Make sure he knows he can always come to you with anything on his mind without fear of being judged or put down.

- **Respect his individuality:** Encourage his interests, support his passions, and celebrate his unique personality.

To have open and honest talks with your son, you need to create a space where he feels comfortable sharing his thoughts and feelings. This means letting go of the need to solve his problems, give advice, or correct him and instead focusing on listening and understanding.

Starting a conversation can feel daunting, especially if your son tends to be reserved. **Here are some tips to get the dialogue flowing:**

- **Start with observations:** "I noticed you've been quiet today. Is everything okay?"

- **Use open-ended questions:** "What was the best part of your day?" "What are you excited about this week?"

- **Share your stories:** "Back when I was your age, I used to..."

- **Create opportunities for conversation:** Do things together that naturally lead to conversation, like taking a walk, playing a game, or cooking.

Fostering open communication is a process that takes patience, consistency, and a readiness to meet your son where he's at. It's about fostering a family culture where feelings are acknowledged, respected, and valued.

By cultivating presence, practicing active listening, responding with empathy, and creating a safe space for talking, you lay the foundation for a strong and lasting connection with your son. This connection will serve as a source of strength and support as he faces life's ups and downs, helping him to embrace his emotional self, build healthy relationships, and thrive in every aspect of his life.

The Power of Presence: Active Listening and Empathy

Imagine your son coming to you; he's frustrated after a disagreement with a friend. At that moment, you have a choice. You can half-listen, offering a distracted "Uh-huh" while scrolling through your phone, or you can choose presence. Put down the phone, face him, and give him your full attention. This is what it means to be truly present – a priceless gift that tells your boy, "You're the most important thing to me right now. I'm all ears, ready to get where you're coming from."

Being present is more than just being in the same room; it's an active engagement with your son's inner world. It's about making eye contact that says, "I'm interested," picking up on the things he's not speaking with his words and listening with all you've got. It's about silencing all the noise in your head and creating space for his emotions to unfold.

When your boy senses that you're fully with him, he feels noticed and important. He gets that his thoughts and emotions matter to you, which gives him a safe zone to be his true self without any worry that you'll judge or ignore him.

Active listening is the foundation of being present.

It's a kind of listening that digs deeper than just the words, reaching for the feelings underneath. It's about repeating what you're hearing, showing that you get his emotions, and asking questions that don't have a simple answer, pushing him to dive deeper into his story.

- **"You seem upset by what your friend said."** This simple reflection shows you're not just catching his words but also tuning into the feelings behind them.

- **"I get why you'd be mad about that."** This kind of response shows you think his feelings are fair, even if you don't see eye to eye on what he did.

- **"Can you tell me more about what went down?"** This kind of question gives him the opportunity to share his side without feeling like he must have the "right" answer.

Empathy is what builds the bridge from your heart to his. It's about putting yourself in his shoes, feeling the world as he does, and getting his emotions even if you've never been in the same boat.

When you respond with empathy, you build a strong connection. You show him you care, you get it, and you're there to back him up, no matter what life throws at you both.

- **"I can only imagine how let down you must've felt."** This tells him you're not just hearing his disappointment but also getting why he feels that way.

- **"It's normal to feel frustrated. We all do at times."** This reassures him that his feelings are normal and that he's not the only one who feels this way.

Being present, listening actively, and showing empathy – these are the things that knit a tight, lasting bond between you and your boy. They lay down a solid base of trust, understanding, and respect, giving him the strength to deal with his feelings with courage and resilience.

Creating a Safe Space for Emotional Expression

Imagine a home filled with laughter, a place where tears are met with comfort and where sharing worries and fears is encouraged without a second thought. This is the kind of haven we aim to build for our sons—a place where their emotional expression is not just tolerated but welcomed and nurtured.

To craft this haven, we start with open arms. It's about shedding old ideas about how boys "ought" to act or feel. It means accepting their full emotions, from joy to sadness, anger to fear. When we receive their feelings without judgment, we give them the green light to be their true selves.

Then there's trust, a cornerstone of this foundation. When your boy knows he can spill his heart out to you without a hint of mockery or scorn, he'll be more inclined to let you into his private world. This trust is cemented through understanding, attentive listening, and honoring his personal space. It's about showing him his emotions are important, that you're ready to listen without critique, and that you'll always be there for him.

Creating a safe space also involves setting clear boundaries. While we encourage emotional expression, teaching the right ways to channel those feelings is crucial. This involves steering him away from harmful reactions like shouting, hitting, or shutting down and toward positive expressions like talking, creating art, or getting active.

Sometimes, simply being there is all it takes to foster this safe space. It's about providing a shoulder to lean on when the world gets too heavy, sitting beside him in quiet solidarity when words escape us, and offering a hug to remind him he's not alone. It's about showing up for him, no matter what.

In this safe space, being open and vulnerable is celebrated as courage. It's a chance to bond more deeply, to peek into his heart, and give him the support he needs to face life's hurdles with resilience and confidence.

Key Points

- **Presence is Powerful:** Being present with your son, both physically and emotionally, is the foundation of a deep bond between parent and child. It means offering him your complete focus, ensuring he feels heard and seen.

- **Active Listening Builds Trust:** When you practice active listening, you're not just hearing his words but understanding the emotions and needs behind them. It shows your son that his thoughts and feelings matter, fostering open communication and trust.

- **Empathy Creates Safety:** Responding with empathy creates an environment where your son can share his feelings without fear of criticism. This not only affirms his feelings but also fortifies the emotional ties between you.

- **Building Bonds Takes Time:** A strong parent-child bond requires ongoing effort. It's nurtured through dedicated time together, displays of affection, honoring each other's uniqueness, and providing a secure place for emotional expression.

- **Open Communication is a Two-Way Street:** To encourage a culture of open communication within the family, it's essential to initiate discussions, listen without preconceptions, and share your own stories. This reciprocal communication is the essence of a healthy family dynamic.

Self-Reflection Questions

1. How frequently do you give your son your attention? What usually pulls your attention away, and what strategies can you implement to be fully there for him?

_____

_____

_____

_____

_____

2. What is your usual reaction when your son opens up about his emotions? Are you an empathetic listener who acknowledges his feelings, or do you often jump in with solutions or advice?

_____

_____

_____

_____

_____

3. What are some activities that you and your son both enjoy? How can you plan more of these fun moments to strengthen your connection?

_____

_____

_____

_____

_____

4. How safe does your son feel expressing himself with you? Is he comfortable sharing his joys and struggles without fear of judgment or criticism?

_____

_____

_____

_____

_____

5. What are some ways you can improve your communication with your son? What can you do to initiate conversations and foster a more profound understanding?

_____

_____

_____

_____

_____

Transformative Exercises

- Create a routine where family meals are electronic devices-free zones. Use this opportunity to connect, share stories, and engage in meaningful conversations.

- Go for a walk together without distractions. Use this time to talk, listen, and connect serenely.

- Decorate a jar and fill it with paper slips containing emotion words or open-ended questions (e.g., **"How's your day going?"** or **"What brings you joy?"**). Take turns drawing a slip and share your thoughts.

- Set aside 15-20 minutes daily for one-on-one time with your son. Let him choose the activity while you give him your attention and participation.

- Before bed each night, share three things you're grateful for with each other. This practice fosters positive emotions and strengthens your relationship.

Chapter 3: Navigating Anger: From Meltdowns to Management

"Speak when you are angry and you will make the best speech you will ever regret." - Ambrose Bierce

Anger is a deep-rooted and intense feeling that we all experience. It's a burst of vitality, a passionate reaction to what we see as threats, unfairness, or irritations. For boys, this intense emotion can be particularly tough to handle, often leading to outbursts that leave them confused and sometimes embarrassed.

Think of a volcano that's quietly rumbling away. The pressure from the lava inside builds up until it can't be contained any longer, resulting in a dramatic eruption that changes the landscape. Similarly, boys' anger can accumulate from various sources, simmering until it overflows in a powerful wave of feelings. Understanding these sources is crucial to helping them deal with their anger positively.

One major factor is physiological. Boys, particularly during adolescence, experience a surge of hormones, including testosterone, which can heighten emotional intensity and impulsivity. Their brains, particularly the part that's in charge of making decisions and controlling impulses, are still maturing. This means they might react angrily before thinking about the consequences.

Growing up also impacts boys. Little boys might show their anger with tantrums or aggressive behavior as they claim independence and test limits. As they age, societal pressures and expectations can fuel anger, especially if they feel inadequate or unable to meet those expectations.

What happens around them is equally important. Witnessing anger in their homes, communities, or even the media can influence how a boy perceives rage and how it's expressed. If they see anger as a standard way to handle disagreements or show power, they might be more inclined to copy that behavior.

Personal experiences, such as going through trauma, being bullied, or learning difficulties, can also make anger more intense. A boy who's been through a lot might be more sensitive to specific triggers and quicker to respond with anger as a way to protect themselves.

Understanding these diverse sources of anger helps us tackle anger management with more empathy. It's not about suppressing anger but giving them the tools to understand, express, and manage it constructively.

Imagine we're putting together a toolkit filled with strategies and techniques to handle anger effectively. One essential tool is de-escalation. When anger starts to heat up, it's crucial to help boys cool off before things get too hot. **This could involve:**

- **Creating space:** Encourage him to take a break from the situation and find a peaceful, relaxing spot.

- **Breathing exercises:** Show him simple breathing techniques to slow his heartbeat and regain control.

- **Physical activity:** Encourage him to work off that built-up energy with exercise, like running, jumping, or playing sports.

- **Sensory input:** Offer calming sensory activities, like listening to gentle music, squeezing a stress ball, or spending time outdoors.

Once the initial intensity subsides, it's time to concentrate on self-control. This involves teaching boys to spot the signs of their anger, figure out what sets it off, and devise ways to cope. **Some practical strategies are:**

- **Identifying anger signs:** Help him notice the physical and emotional signs of anger, like clenched fists, racing heart, or feeling hot.

- **Self-talk:** Encourage him to challenge angry thoughts with positive self-talk and replace them with more helpful ones.

- **Problem-solving:** Teach him to identify the problem that made him angry and brainstorm potential solutions.

- **Mindfulness:** Introduce mindfulness practices, like meditation or focused attention, to help him become more mindful of his feelings and thoughts in the moment.

Expressing anger healthily is crucial. It's natural to feel angry, but teaching boys how to show their anger is essential. **Here's how to help them:**

- **Assertive communication:** Show him how to clearly and respectfully express his needs and concerns, using "I" statements (e.g., "I feel angry when...")

- **Creative expression:** Encourage him to direct his anger into creative pursuits, such as writing, drawing, music, or sports.

- **Peaceful conflict resolution:** Give him the skills to resolve conflicts without fighting, like active listening, finding middle ground, and finding solutions that work for everyone.

Remember, managing anger is a process, not a one-time thing. There will be ups and downs along the way. But with patient coaching and ongoing encouragement, you can help your son learn the skills he needs to handle anger positively, turning it into a force for personal growth and change.

Understanding the Roots of Anger in Boys

Anger doesn't just pop up out of nowhere—it's a complex emotion that signals more going on beneath the surface. To help boys deal with their anger, we've got to dig into what's causing it, the stuff lighting the fuse for those explosive moments.

Think about it like a detective, carefully piecing together the evidence to figure out what's behind those heated feelings. Sometimes, the cause is apparent – a frustrating situation, feeling wronged, or a need that's not being met. But a lot of times, it's more complicated, with all sorts of things like body changes, growing pains, and what's happening around them all getting mixed in.

Teenage boys have all these hormones zooming around, cranking up their emotions so it feels like they're on a wild ride. Their brains are still wired up, especially the parts that help them think before they act, which can make them snap in anger quickly.

As boys grow up, anger can mean different things. Younger boys might get mad to assert independence, test boundaries, or when they can't get what they want. Older boys might feel the heat when stressed about fitting in or living up to what's expected of them.

The environment they grow up in also plays a significant role. If they see anger used to resolve conflicts or assert dominance, they might think that's the way to go. Seeing too much violence around them in real life or the media can make it seem normal.

Past experiences—like dealing with bullies, trauma, or struggling at school—can leave marks that make them get angry quickly as a way to protect themselves.

Getting the complete picture of where anger comes from helps us be more understanding and thoughtful about handling it. It's not just about slapping on an "angry" label—it's about seeing that their anger is often a clue to deeper needs, hurdles, or past hurts.

Teaching Healthy Anger Expression and Coping Strategies

Picture this: A young boy standing at a crossroads. One path leads to a volcanic eruption of anger, with harsh words flying like daggers and actions causing havoc. The other path leads to a serene place where anger is acknowledged, understood, and channeled constructively. We, as parents, can guide our sons toward this path by showing them how to express and handle their anger healthily.

It's akin to learning a new language – the language of healthy anger expression. Instead of erupting in shouts and door-slamming, we can teach boys to articulate their feelings with words. Saying "I feel angry because..." can be a game-changer, allowing them to vent without falling into aggression or spiteful words.

This new language is about pinpointing what sets off their anger. Could it be a particular event, someone's actions, or a need that's not being met? Knowing what sparks their ire gives them the upper hand, allowing them to spot the warning signs and tackle their anger before it escalates.

Just like a firefighter has a toolkit for different emergencies, boys can master various techniques to keep their anger in check. Deep breathing can be their go-to like a fire hose cooling down the flames of fury. Exercise can serve as their axe, chopping away the built-up energy and stress. A quiet spot becomes their fire extinguisher, smothering the flames before they turn into a wildfire.

Learning to express anger healthily and positively is similar to learning to play an instrument. Initially, it might not sound good. But with time and mentoring, they can learn to play out their feelings in a tune that's both impactful and harmonious.

This might involve channeling their anger into creative outlets, like writing, drawing, or playing music. It could mean engaging in physical activities that burn off steam, such as jogging, swimming, or team sports. Or it might involve picking up skills for sorting out conflicts, like listening to others, finding a middle ground, and aiming for solutions that everyone's happy with.

It's crucial to remember that teaching boys to express anger healthily isn't about stifling the anger or pretending it's not there. It's about acknowledging that anger is a natural emotion, but showing how it's expressed matters. It's about equipping them with the tools to manage their anger positively so it doesn't end up controlling them.

Key Points

- **Anger is a Multifaceted Emotion:** Anger in boys stems from a complex interplay of physiological factors (hormones, brain development), developmental stages, environmental influences, and individual experiences.

- **De-escalation Cools the Flames:** When anger rises, de-escalation techniques like creating space, deep breathing, physical activity, and sensory input can help boys chill out before an outburst.

- **Mastering Emotions Through Self-Control:** Learning to manage anger means spotting the warning signs, pinpointing what sets it off, and honing skills such as talking to oneself, problem-solving, and mindfulness to keep anger in check.

- **Expressing Anger the Right Way:** Anger is a natural emotion, but how it's shown counts. Teaching boys to speak up, channel their feelings through creativity, and navigate disagreements skillfully encourages positive ways to let it out.

- **Anger Management is a Journey:** Helping boys manage anger is a relentless task that demands understanding, a helping hand, and the flexibility to switch up approaches as they evolve.

Self-Reflection Questions

1. How do you express anger? How do you handle frustration, and could this be shaping how your son deals with his anger?

_____

_____

_____

_____

_____

2. What sets your son off? Are specific situations, people, or unmet needs provoking his anger? What strategies could you teach him to prepare for and manage these anger?

_____

_____

_____

_____

_____

3. What is the tactic you use to manage your anger? Are there any techniques among these that your son could benefit from learning and putting into practice?

_____

_____

_____

_____

_____

4. What's your response when your son gets angry? Are you escalating the situation, or do you remain calm and offer support?

_____

_____

_____

_____

_____

5. How can you create an environment conducive to learning and practicing anger expression healthily for your son? What resources or tools might be helpful to him?

_____

_____

_____

_____

_____

Transformative Exercises

- Create a visual representation of anger levels, from calm to enraged. Help your son identify his anger cues and monitor his anger levels as the day passes.

- Put together a kit with items that can soothe your son when he feels anger bubbling up, like a stress ball, a favorite book, calming music, or a soft blanket.

- Encourage your son to keep a journal to track his anger episodes, noting what sets him off, how intense it felt, the techniques he used to calm down, and how things turned out. This will boost his self-awareness and help him identify patterns.

- Practice scenarios that could provoke anger and discuss various ways to handle those moments with assertiveness and respect.

- Create a family agreement outlining acceptable ways to express anger and strategies for resolving conflicts peacefully. This will help build a mutual understanding and commitment to managing anger constructively.

Chapter 4: Taming Anxiety: Calming the Storms Within

"Our anxiety does not come from thinking about the future,
but from wanting to control it." - Kahlil Gibran

Anxiety, that pervasive feeling of worry, nervousness, or unease, can overshadow a boy's life. It pops up in various ways—sometimes subtle and hidden, other times erupting in a storm of physical and emotional distress. Spotting the signs of anxiety in boys is crucial to helping them get through these rough patches.

Anxiety isn't like a bruise or a fever. It's sneakier than that, often working behind the scenes, filling a boy's head with doubts and fears that slowly destroy his confidence and well-being. You might notice him pulling back from friends or ditching hobbies he used to love. His sleep could be a mess, with worries keeping him up and restless. Or maybe he's often got a stomachache or a headache—those can be the physical side effects of the stress he's feeling inside.

In other cases, anxiety is right there in your face. He might snap or get angry at the drop of a hat, especially when things get too much for him. He might struggle to concentrate in school, his mind preoccupied with worries and stuck on a loop of "what-ifs." Or he might need to hear that everything's alright repeatedly.

Telling the difference between everyday kid worries and the more intense kind of anxiety isn't always easy. It's normal for kids to be anxious at some point, whether it's about a test, a party, or even a change in routine. Those worries usually come and go. But when anxiety sticks around, gets out of hand, and starts messing with a kid's day-to-day life, that's when you know it's time to step in and offer a helping hand.

If you see your son struggling with anxiety, remember to be kind and understanding. Don't brush off his concerns or tell him just to chill out. Instead, let him know it's okay to talk about what's bugging him and ensure he knows you're there to listen and help without judgment.

Think of yourself as his cheerleader in the game of emotions, helping him build skills to tackle his anxiety. Start with some relaxation tricks to help cool down his body's alarm bells, like slowing his heartbeat, loosening up his muscles, and bringing on a peaceful vibe.

Teaching him to breathe deeply can make a big difference. Have him take slow, deep breaths to fill up his lungs and let them out gently. This simple act can help regulate his nervous system and reduce feelings of overwhelm.

Progressive muscle relaxation is another helpful technique. It involves tensing up and relaxing different muscles, which can help him chill out and reduce his anxiety.

Visualization exercises can also be effective. Get him to picture a relaxing scene, like a quiet beach or his favorite hangout spot. It's a great way to get his mind off the worries and into a more peaceful state.

Mindfulness practices are another valuable tool to have up his sleeve. It's all about staying focused on the now without stressing about it. It keeps his mind off fretting about tomorrow or regretting yesterday, and just being in the moment.

Simple things like focusing on his breathing can help keep him anchored in the present, which can help push those anxious thoughts away.

Mindful walking is another cool trick. It involves paying attention to the sensations of walking – the feel of his feet hitting the ground, the way his body moves, and all the stuff he sees and hears around him. It's a way to connect with the world and stay present.

Mindful eating is about enjoying every bite, really getting into the flavors, textures, and smells. It can make mealtime more about the food and less about the anxiety that can sometimes come with it.

Then, there are ways to tackle those anxious thoughts head-on. These strategies help guys notice when they're falling into negative thinking traps, question those thoughts, and swap them out for something more positive and realistic.

Questioning his thoughts means he'll learn to look for the actual evidence behind his worries. Ask himself questions like, "What's the evidence here? Can I see this another way? What would I say to a friend who was having this thought?"

Positive self-talk is about switching out those downer thoughts with some good vibes. He can pump himself up with phrases like "I've got this," "I'm strong," or "I'm on it."

Problem-solving is about breaking down overwhelming problems into bite-sized chunks. Encourage your son to figure out the problem, brainstorm solutions, and then make a plan to deal with it step-by-step.

Remember, every boy is unique, and what works for one may not work for another. Try out various relaxation methods, mindfulness practices, and cognitive strategies to find out what helps your son manage his anxiety most effectively.

By giving him these tools and standing by him, you're setting him up to master his anxiety. You're helping him grow more robust, gain confidence, and face life's ups and downs with much more chill.

Recognizing the Signs of Anxiety in Boys

Anxiety in boys can often be sneaky, changing its appearance and blending into the background. It can disguise itself as irritability, stomach pains, or a sudden lack of interest in things they used to love. Spotting these varied clues is vital to give your son the help he needs.

At times, anxiety can be loud, with a pounding heart, sweaty hands, and a queasy belly. These physical symptoms might come with fear, too much worrying, or a sense of being swamped. Your son might complain of headaches, muscle tension, or difficulty sleeping, which are all signs that anxiety is weighing him down.

Other times, anxiety might be sneakier, revealing itself through small changes in how he acts. He may start to pull back from friends or hobbies he used to like. He might be unable to stay still or focus or need lots of reassurance that things are alright.

Keep an eye on his emotional landscape. Anxiety often brings a cloud of fear, worry, and self-doubt. He might worry too much about what's to come, keep thinking about things he messed up, or try too hard to be perfect. He could get cranky or have sudden mood swings, which are signs of the stress he's dealing with inside.

Spotting the signs of anxiety is like cracking a secret code. It's about understanding the small signals and undercover messages that reveal the presence of this often-misunderstood emotion.

Building Resilience and Coping Mechanisms for Anxiety

Think of resilience as a robust ship navigating stormy seas. It yields with the waves, adjusts its sails, and stays the course even as winds howl. When we teach resilience to boys, we're preparing them to face life's anxious moments not by dodging them but by developing the strength and skills to navigate them confidently.

Fostering a growth mindset is one approach to building resilience. Urge your son to view obstacles as chances for personal development and learning, not as hazards. Help him understand that setbacks are not failures but stepping stones on the path to success.

Coping mechanisms are like the lifeboats on this resilient ship, offering support and safety when the seas get rough. These tools and strategies help boys handle anxiety and restore tranquility when feelings start to bubble up.

Deep breathing is an anchor, grounding them in the present moment and calming their racing thoughts. Exercise becomes a life raft, carrying them away from the tumultuous waves being worried and towards the calmer shores of physical exertion. Mindfulness becomes a compass that guides them back to the present moment when they're lost in the stormy waters of "what-ifs."

Cognitive reframing is akin to adjusting the sails, helping them to tilt their viewpoint and perceive challenges in a new light. Instead of dwelling on the negatives, they learn to spot the positives, the opportunities for growth, and the lessons learned.

These coping tools aren't universally applicable; what's effective for one boy might not suit another. The aim is to assist your son in uncovering suitable techniques and strategies and make him feel capable of tackling his anxiety and taking on life's hurdles with more resilience and confidence.

Key Points

- **Anxiety Takes Many Forms:** Boys might show signs of anxiety with stomach aches or headaches and changes in how they act, such as becoming easily upset and feeling worried or scared.

- **Recognizing the Red Flags:** It's important to tell the difference between worries and anxiety that requires attention and support. Look for worry that's constant and intense enough to interfere with everyday activities.

- **Relaxation Techniques Calm the Body:** Practices like taking deep breaths, relaxing your muscles, and picturing peaceful scenes can help control the body's reaction to stress.

- **Mindfulness Grounds in the Present:** Engaging in mindfulness, such as breathing, walking, and eating, can help keep your mind from drifting to past or future worries.

- **Cognitive Strategies Reframe Thoughts:** Cognitive techniques, such as questioning anxious thoughts, talking about oneself positively, and solving problems, can help boys identify and reframe anxious thoughts.

Self-Reflection Questions

1. What's your response when you feel anxious? Do you avoid situations that make you nervous or tackle them directly? How might your approach be influencing your son?

_____

_____

_____

_____

_____

2. How aware are you of your son's anxiety levels? Can you pick up on the little changes in his acts that could show he's anxious?

_____

_____

_____

_____

_____

3. What do you do to calm down when you're stressed or anxious? Do you think any of these methods could also benefit your son?

_____

_____

_____

_____

_____

4. How often do you practice mindfulness? Do you think making mindfulness a part of your family's daily life could help your son feel more at ease?

_____

_____

_____

_____

_____

5. When your son is worried or has negative thoughts, how do you support him in overcoming them? Do you encourage him to challenge his fears and consider different viewpoints?

_____

_____

_____

_____

_____

Transformative Exercises

- Decorate a box and suggest that your son jot down any concerns on little pieces of paper and place them in the box. It is a way to externalize worries and create a sense of control.

- Set a one-minute timer each day to engage in calm breathing exercises together. Pay attention to how the breath flows in and out, and let that be your focus.

- Go for a walk together and swap stories about what you both appreciate. This practice nudges your minds towards the good stuff, dialing down the anxious vibes.

- Encourage your son to stand before a mirror every morning and speak some encouraging words to himself, like "I'm courageous," "I've got this," or "I'm up for the challenge."

- Sketch a chart with space for pinpointing the issue, brainstorming solutions, and creating an action plan. Use this chart to help your son break down overwhelming problems into bite-sized pieces he can tackle.

Chapter 5: Confronting Sadness and Depression

"The bravest thing I ever did was continuing my life when I wanted to die." - Juliette Lewis

Sadness is part of being human; we all feel it when faced with setbacks or troubles. It's like a wave that engulfs us, leaving a trace of melancholy and introspection. However, when this sadness doesn't fade and starts to cast a long shadow over a young man's life, it could be a sign of something more profound: depression.

Unfortunately, depression in boys is often hidden because of stigma. Society's views on what it means to be "masculine" can make it hard for them to share their feelings of sadness or depression. They might worry about being seen as weak or imperfect.

This stigma can be harmful. Boys battling with depression might pull away from those they love, isolate themselves in their rooms, or find unhealthy ways to deal with their pain. They may struggle in school, lose interest in things they used to like, or they might even think about hurting themselves.

It is important to spot these warning signs in boys. While it's normal to feel sad, depression is a severe issue that needs care and support. Keep in mind that depression can look different in boys than in girls. Boys might hide their depression behind anger, irritability, or risky behaviors.

Some signs to watch out for in boys include:

- **Constant sadness or irritability:** A mood that seems consistently low or quickly turns to anger.

- **Not caring about fun stuff:** Not wanting to do hobbies, sports, or hang out with friends.

- **Sleeping issues:** Difficulty falling asleep, staying asleep, or sleeping too much.

- **Changes in appetite:** Loss of appetite or overeating.

- **Fatigue or energy loss:** Being tired always, even with enough sleep.

- **Difficulty concentrating:** Having difficulty paying attention at school or with tasks.

- **Feeling worthless or guilty:** Negative self-talk or blaming oneself too much.

- **Thinking about death or suicide:** Talking about dying or having thoughts about it.

If you see these signs in your son, approach him with empathy and concern. Let him know you've noticed he's different and that you're concerned. Make a space where he can talk freely without being judged. Listen well and let him know his feelings are valid and you're there to support him.

Helping a son through tough times means using different strategies. One crucial step is to get professional help. A therapist can offer him a space to talk about his feelings, learn how to deal with them, and get treatment.

Talking openly is also essential. Encourage him to talk about his feelings, even if it's tough. Show him you'll listen without judging and want to help him feel better. Don't brush off his feelings or give simple fixes. Instead, validate what he's going through and offer constant support.

Creating a supportive environment is essential for his recovery. This means making a place where he feels secure, loved, and accepted. Promote healthy habits like exercise, eating well, and sleeping enough. Connect him with positive activities and friends. Celebrate what he's good at and his successes, reminding him of his value.

By breaking down the stigma, spotting the signs, getting professional help, keeping communication open, and making a nurturing environment, you can give your son the strength to face depression with bravery and hope. You can help him find his happiness again, remember his strengths, and create a hopeful, bright future.

Breaking the Stigma: Recognizing Depression in Boys

Imagine an unseen heavyweight weighing down a boy's shoulders. It's the heavy load of stigma, the unspoken belief that boys must always be stoic, that tears and emotional struggles are off-limits for them. This stigma, when it comes to depression in boys, can seriously block their path to seeking aid and getting better.

Breaking this stigma starts with understanding. Depression isn't about being weak or having personal faults; it's a severe mental health issue that impacts countless boys all over the globe. Think of it as an illness, much like any physical one, that demands understanding, care, and a supportive hand.

Spotting depression in boys can be tricky because it often hides behind masks of anger, irritability, or risky behaviors. They may lash out in vexation, pull back from loved ones, or dive into dangerous pastimes to dull their inner turmoil. These actions are calls for help, red flags that something deeper is wrong.

You've got to look beyond the surface. Be mindful of the little signs – the downcast eyes, the silence, the sudden disinterest in hobbies that used to bring joy. Hear the words they aren't saying, the heavy sighs, the utterances of hopelessness. These are the faint cries of depression, pleading to be recognized and understood.

Breaking the stigma is also about fostering a space where boys feel safe sharing their struggles. Assure them it's perfectly fine to feel down and that reaching out for support reflects bravery, not frailty. Affirm their emotions, offer support, and reassure them they're not fighting alone.

By smashing the stigma that clings to depression in boys, we pave the way for healing and recovery. We encourage them to seek help, share their burdens, and reclaim their lives from this debilitating illness.

Supporting a Son Struggling with Sadness and Depression

Imagine your son as a young plant in the middle of a storm. The wind whips at his branches, the rain weighs down his leaves, and the darkness threatens to engulf him. As his parent, you stand as the solid pillar, the refuge that shields him from the storm and the nourishing daylight that aids his growth.

Being there for your son when he's struggling with sorrow and depression requires steadfast affection, patience, and understanding. It's about being a constant figure in his life, a haven where he can find solace amid emotional upheavals.

Start by hearing him out. When he opens up, even if it's a subtle hint of gloom or a slight sign of distress, hear him without passing judgment. Affirm his emotions, reassuring him it's alright to feel this way, that you understand his pain, and that you're here to help him through it.

Celebrate his small victories. Depression can make it difficult to see the good and to appreciate the small accomplishments. Pay attention to his efforts, acknowledge his progress, and remind him of his capabilities.

Keep in mind that helping your son through sadness and depression is a journey that requires patience and perseverance. There will be obstacles and setbacks. But with your love and support, he can emerge through the hardship, reclaim his vigor, and unfold into the remarkable person he's destined to become.

Key Points

- **Depression is a serious health issue:** It's crucial to understand that depression isn't a sign of weakness; it's a medical condition that affects boys just as it does to girls.

- **Stigma Hinders Seeking for Help:** Often, societal norms and false beliefs about what it means to be 'masculine' can stop boys from admitting they're struggling with depression and from getting the help they need.

- **Depression can look different in boys:** Instead of sadness, boys might hide their depressive feelings behind anger, irritability, risky behaviors, or withdrawal, making it crucial to spot these less apparent signs.

- **Getting Professional Help is Vital:** Mental health professionals, like therapists and counselors, are equipped to offer tailored assistance, teach effective coping techniques, and provide treatments grounded in research for managing depression.

- **Supportive Environments Aids Recovery:** Creating a safe, supportive, and non-judgmental environment at home, along with encouraging healthy habits and celebrating strengths, is crucial for recovery.

Self-Reflection Questions

1. What are your personal views and feelings about depression? Have you noticed any preconceived notions or misunderstandings that could hinder being there for your son?

_____

_____

_____

_____

_____

2. How comfortable are you when it comes to discussing feelings and mental health matters with your son? How do you go about making these discussions more open and welcoming?

_____

_____

_____

_____

_____

3. How well do you spot the symptoms of depression? Are you aware of how depression might look different in boys?

_____

_____

_____

_____

_____

4. What kind of support systems for mental health do you have access to in your area? Do you know the steps to take to seek professional guidance when it's necessary?

_____

_____

_____

_____

_____

5. What steps can you take to make your home a warmer and more encouraging place for your son? What adjustments can be made to help nurture his emotional health?

_____

_____

_____

_____

_____

Transformative Exercises

- Make it a habit to check in with your son about his emotional well-being regularly. This could be through a casual chat, journal writing, or an app to track his moods.

- Encourage your son to identify his strengths and the things he's done well, no matter how small. You could start a "strength jar" where he can jot down his good traits and achievements.

- Do good deeds together, like volunteering, lending a hand to a neighbor, or giving to a charity. These actions can lift spirits and provide a sense of purpose.

- Try mindfulness exercises together, like deep breathing, listening to soothing tunes, or spending time in nature. These can help reduce stress and bring composure.

- Put together a list of reliable relatives, pals, or mentors who are there to back up and cheer on your son. Knowing a circle of folks who care can make a world of difference.

Chapter 6: Fostering Self-Awareness and Emotional Literacy

"The most terrifying thing is to accept oneself completely." -
Carl Jung

Self-awareness is the inner guide that helps us understand who we are. It's recognizing our strengths and areas for improvement and grasping what drives us. For boys, developing self-awareness is akin to shining a spotlight on the inner workings of their emotions, bringing clarity to their highs and lows.

Conversely, emotional literacy is how we articulate those deep-seated feelings. We can pinpoint, grasp, and share our emotions effectively through words or body language. Picture an artist with a vibrant array of paints without a brush to bring their vision to life. In the same way, a boy might find himself brimming with complex emotions but struggle to express them, leading to frustration and sometimes rocky relationships.

Guiding boys in growing their self-awareness and emotional literacy is like handing them the tools to traverse the intricate landscape of their feelings. It equips them to get to know themselves better, interact more effectively, and form solid connections.

Helping boys recognize and name their emotions is crucial in this process. Often, boys are taught to describe their feelings with basic terms like "happy," "sad," or "mad." By broadening their emotional vocabulary, we're expanding their color palette, enabling them to convey their feelings' more delicate and complex aspects.

So, instead of just saying "mad," they can discern between feeling frustrated, angry, annoyed, or peeved. Rather than simply "sad," they can explore feelings like disappointment, sorrow, loneliness, or a sense of deep reflection. This language helps them share their emotions with more detail and clarity.

But there's more to self-awareness than just naming emotions. It's about grasping the "why" behind what they feel. What sets off their feelings of anger or worry? Which deeper needs or beliefs are at play in their emotional reactions? Encouraging boys to reflect through journaling, sketching, or chatting can help them probe deeper into their emotional lives.

Creative activities can be mighty allies in this quest for self-awareness. Crafting a "feelings wheel" with various emotions depicted in colors can aid boys in pinpointing and understanding their feelings. Using art as an expression can give them a silent yet powerful means to explore and convey their emotions. Penning poems or stories about their feelings can offer them a way to work through emotions and discover more about themselves.

Teaching boys healthy ways to express their emotions is just as crucial. This means steering them toward sharing their feelings assertively and with respect, steering clear of aggression, withdrawal, or other negative coping strategies.

Verbal expression is essential. We can encourage boys to talk about their feelings using "I" statements, which keeps the focus on their own experiences rather than pointing fingers at others. For instance, swapping "You make me mad" with "I feel mad when..." helps them take ownership of their emotions and paves the way for more positive conversations.

Body language, facial expressions, and tone of voice are critical pieces of the puzzle. Making boys more aware of these silent signals can sharpen their communication skills and dodge potential mix-ups.

Role-playing can be a handy practice, too. It lets boys try out how to share feelings like anger or sadness in a fantastic, collected way. This practice gives them a safe space to find their voice and the confidence to express themselves genuinely.

Helping Boys Identify and Name Their Emotions

Picture a young boy gazing at the night sky, mesmerized by the countless stars. Each star has a name, a place, and a story to tell. Similarly, the emotions swirling within a boy's heart are like a constellation of feelings, each with its unique identity and significance.

Guiding boys to recognize and articulate their feelings is akin to handing them a cosmic map for their inner space. It's all about equipping them with the language and tools to recognize, understand, and articulate the vast array of feelings that make up their emotional landscape.

Kick things off by broadening their emotions. Step beyond the simple tags like "happy," "sad," or "angry." Introduce a broader spectrum of emotions such as exhilaration, vexation, letdown, nervousness, pride, thankfulness, and curiosity. The more terminology they possess for their sentiments, the more precise their expression can be.

Leverage the little moments in daily life as teaching opportunities. If your boy gets frustrated while building a tower, help him name that feeling. Help him put a name to that emotion. When he glows pridefully from a well-earned goal, cheer on his joy and thrill. If he's tense about an upcoming test, acknowledge his concerns and explain his anxiety.

Urge him to be mindful of his physical responses. Emotions often manifest physically. A racing heart could be a sign of fright or exhilaration. A clenched jaw might indicate anger or tension. Assist him in drawing the line between these clues and their emotional counterparts.

Craft a "feelings chart" with pictures or drawings representing different emotions. This tool can aid him in pinpointing and naming his emotions, particularly when words elude him.

Bear in mind that guiding boys to identify and articulate their emotions isn't about pressing them to dissect every sentiment or over analyze their encounters. It's about providing them with the tools and language to understand their inner world, communicate their needs effectively, and tackle life's hurdles with greater self-awareness and emotional intelligence.

Developing Emotional Vocabulary and Expression

Imagine a young boy trying to describe a gorgeous sunset using just "red" and "yellow." Sure, he'd get the gist across, but the full array of colors, the dance of light and shadows, and the sheer wonder of it all would be lost in translation. In the same way, when a boy has a limited emotional vocabulary, he can't share the whole picture of what's stirring inside him.

Expanding his emotional vocabulary is like handing him a new set of colors to illustrate his feelings. Instead of just saying "happy" or "sad," he can learn to express a range of emotions like joy, excitement, contentment, delight, disappointment, grief, loneliness, and melancholy.

With this broader set of terms, he can pinpoint and communicate his feelings with more accuracy and detail. It's like giving him the tools to spot the subtle differences in his emotions, get his own experiences, and forge deeper connections with others around him.

However, developing emotional vocabulary is not just about memorizing a list of fancy words. It's about making it okay for him to dive into those feelings and talk about them without worrying about being judged or embarrassed. It means cheering him on to use those words to articulate what he needs, what scares him, what he's hoping for, and what he dreams about.

Talking about feelings is like building a bridge from his heart to the world outside. It's his ticket to sharing his story, making friends, and handling social scenes with more poise and confidence.

And hey, it's not all about the words. Things like gestures, facial expressions, and how he says stuff can also pack a ton of emotional meaning. Guiding him to be in tune with these silent signals can sharpen how he gets his message across and help dodge any misunderstandings.

Teaching a kid to express his emotions through words and actions is like handing him a megaphone for his soul. It's vital to help him know himself better, to grow his emotional smarts, and to equip him with the strength and truthfulness he needs to face life's ups and downs.

Key Points

- **Expand the Emotional Vocabulary:** Guide boys in identifying and articulating their emotions with more precise terms, like "frustrated," "disappointed," or "content," moving beyond just "happy," "sad," or "mad." This helps them grasp the subtleties of their feelings.

- **Create a Judgment-Free Zone:** Make it clear to boys that it's completely fine to share their feelings openly and honestly. Assure them that all emotions are valid and that they won't face criticism for expressing themselves.

- **Encourage Direct Communication:** Show boys the power of "I" statements for sharing their emotions in a direct but considerate way, focusing on their experiences rather than pointing fingers at others.

- **Nonverbal Cues Matter:** Teach boys to pay attention to their body language, facial expressions, and tone of voice. Understanding these nonverbal signals can improve their communication ability and avoid misinterpretations.

- **Practice Makes Progress:** Offer boys various ways to practice expressing their feelings, like through role-playing games, writing in a journal, or engaging in artistic activities. Regular practice can enhance their emotional expression skills.

Self-Reflection Questions

1. Could you describe your emotional vocabulary? Would you say it's broad enough or a bit on the narrow side? How might your vocabulary be influencing your son's?

_____

_____

_____

_____

_____

2. What's your response when your son shows intense emotions? Are you the type to encourage him to put his feelings into words, or do you accidentally put a damper on his emotional expression?

_____

_____

_____

_____

_____

3. How often does your family chat about their feelings? Do you guys make it a point to talk openly and honestly about emotions?

_____

_____

_____

_____

_____

4. How's your son picking up on the unsaid stuff, like facial expressions and the way people hold themselves? Can he decode those silent emotional signals?

_____

_____

_____

_____

_____

5. What kind of approaches could you try to help your son better understand his emotions and express them freely?

_____

_____

_____

_____

_____

Transformative Exercises

- Jot down many feelings on little paper and take turns trying to show that emotion with just your face and body language—no talking allowed! It's a fantastic way for guys to get the hang of what different emotions look like without any words.

- Kick things off with a super simple feeling, like "sad," and then get creative thinking up all sorts of words like "sad" but have their vibe, such as disappointed, lonely, and heartbroken.

- Grab some artsy stuff like crayons, paint, or clay, and encourage your son to let those feelings out by making some art. It's a sweet way to let emotions flow without putting them into words.

- Team up to cook up a story where you both add a sentence and sprinkle in many feelings to spice things up.

- Set aside some time each week for a "feelings meeting" where everyone can share what's been happening with them and how they've been feeling. It's a fab way to make talking about emotions a regular thing and helps everyone get better at chatting about their feelings.

Chapter 7: Cultivating Empathy: Connecting with Others

"Empathy is seeing with the eyes of another, listening with the ears of another, and feeling with the heart of another." -
Alfred Adler

Empathy is the glue that binds us together, enabling us to understand and feel what others are going through. It's a crucial part of being human, a way to leave our shoes and walk a mile in someone else's. For boys, learning to empathize is like opening a window to a broader world, allowing them to see beyond themselves and connect with others on a deeper, more meaningful level.

As boys grow up, empathy blossoms gradually, shaped by their innate tendencies and the nurturing they receive. Even as babies, they start to exhibit empathetic responses, like crying when they hear another baby's cry. As they get older, their brains develop, and they begin to grasp that other people have their thoughts and feelings.

Social experiences play a crucial role in nurturing this growth. Positive interactions with family, friends, and caregivers allow boys to watch and learn about emotions, practice seeing things from another's viewpoint, and develop compassion.

But sometimes, the pressures of society and the "boy code" can put up roadblocks to empathy. Boys are often told to be tough and might feel they shouldn't show they're vulnerable or sensitive. This can lead them to suppress their own emotions and struggle to connect with the feelings of others.

Parents can play a massive role in turning this around and helping their boys grow in empathy. By creating a space where feelings are important and shared freely, we can encourage boys to honor their sensitivity and better understand others.

To teach boys empathy, we need to use a mix of approaches. A big one is leading by example. When we show empathy when dealing with others, we give our sons a real-life template. This could mean talking about our emotions, caring about what others are going through, or doing kind deeds.

Another approach is to encourage them to think about how others feel. Ask your son questions like, "How do you think your buddy felt when that happened?" or "What might be going on for him?"

Sharing stories or watching films can also be a springboard for chats about the emotions and reasons behind characters' actions, which helps build empathy and understanding.

Letting boys get involved in kind acts is another excellent way to grow their empathy. Nudge them to lend a hand, whether helping at a community food bank, giving toys to kids in need, or helping a neighbor. These moments let them connect with others, see their needs, and feel the happiness of giving.

Finally, having open talks about social issues can widen their view and nurture empathy. Discuss what's happening in the world, the unfairness some people face, or the struggles of different groups. Encourage them to look at all sides, ask questions, and develop a sense of compassion for others.

Teaching Boys to Understand and Share Feelings

Imagine teaching a boy how to play a musical instrument. He begins with single notes, advances to chords and melodies, and masters entire symphonies. Similarly, teaching boys to grasp and convey emotions is an incremental journey. It starts with the basics and gradually expands into a more complex emotional spectrum.

Kick things off by helping him identify and label his emotions. Asking, "Are you feeling mad?" or "Are you upset about what went down?" can help him link his feelings to words, laying the groundwork for emotional comprehension and expression.

Then, encourage him to recognize the emotions in others. Queries like, "Can you tell how your buddy is feeling by looking at him?" or "Any idea why she's crying?" enable him to pick up on the nonverbal signals communicating how others feel.

Narratives from books, films, or everyday events are fantastic for exploring emotions. Discuss the emotions, drives, and connections of the characters. Questions like, "What do you think made the character do that?" or "How would that make you feel?" encourage him to see things from different perspectives and enrich his emotional insight.

It's crucial to encourage him to open up about his emotions, the good and the bad. Forge a space where he can express his feelings without worrying about criticism. Be present, affirm what he's going through, and provide your support. This kind of open dialogue fosters trust and fortifies your bond.

Much like a musician who becomes adept at various instruments, boys can learn diverse ways to articulate their emotions. Encourage him to write in a journal, draw, or partake in creative endeavors to express himself. This offers him a gentle approach to probe his emotions and gain self-awareness.

Educating boys on understanding and communicating their feelings is akin to handing them a key to the complex realm of human connections. It equips them to forge sturdier relationships, deftly navigate social contexts, and contribute to a more caring and empathetic world.

Encouraging Perspective-Taking and Compassion

Imagine your son standing on a hilltop, gazing out at the world. Teaching him to take on another's perspective is akin to handing him a telescope, enhancing his ability to peer into the lives of others—to grasp their triumphs and trials with sharper focus.

It's guiding him to grasp that his viewpoint isn't the only one out there and that each person's viewpoint is carved from their own life story and context. This insight lays the foundation for empathy, forging a path for him to engage with people more profoundly and sincerely.

From such understanding, compassion flows naturally. When we genuinely get where someone else is coming from, our hearts can't help but go out to them—whether facing hurdles, celebrating victories, or just being human.

Nurturing this skill involves asking questions that prompt him to consider what others might be thinking or feeling. Questions like, "How do you think your friend felt when you made that comment?" "Can you imagine what it's like walking in her shoes?" These questions encourage him to step beyond his bubble and peek through someone else's lens.

Reading stories together is another potent method to encourage this skill. Discuss the characters' drives, their obstacles, and their sentiments. Encourage your son to put himself in their place and feel alongside them.

Role-play can be another playful yet impactful approach. Swap parts, play out various scenes, and let him directly taste different viewpoints. It's a lively way to build empathy and insight.

Remember, perspective-taking isn't solely about others; it's also about self-awareness. Encourage him to reflect on his thoughts, feelings, and behaviors. Guide him to appreciate how he can affect those around him, nurturing a sense of duty and self-awareness.

Key Points

- **Empathy is a Skill:** Think of empathy as a skill you can develop by making a conscious effort and practicing regularly.

- **Leading by Example:** Kids pick up cues from their surroundings, especially from their parents. When parents consistently show empathy in how they deal with others, it sets a strong, positive example for their boys to emulate.

- **Expanding Views through Others' Eyes:** It's beneficial to urge boys to look at situations from different perspectives and imagine walking in someone else's shoes. This practice nurtures empathy and a caring attitude.

- **Acts of Kindness as Empathy Lessons:** When boys participate in kind deeds and help those in need, they experience the essence of empathy and witness its beneficial effects firsthand.

- **Conversations that Open Minds:** Engaging boys in meaningful discussions about societal issues and various communities' struggles can foster empathy and provide a broader perspective.

Self-Reflection Questions

1. In what ways do you demonstrate empathy in your daily life? Are you someone who gives them full attention, acknowledges their emotions, and extends a helping hand when needed?

_____

_____

_____

_____

_____

2. How regularly do you encourage your son to look at things from another's viewpoint? Do you ask him questions that lead him to consider the emotions someone else might experience in different scenarios?

_____

_____

_____

_____

_____

3. What chances does your son have to be kind and lend a hand to those in need? How might you bring more of these moments into his life?

_____

_____

_____

_____

_____

4. Do you discuss social issues and current events with your son? How can you encourage him to think critically and develop compassion for those who aren't like him?

_____

_____

_____

_____

_____

5. What steps can you take to create a more empathetic environment in your home? Which principles and actions can you promote to encourage a spirit of understanding within your family?

_____

_____

_____

_____

_____

Transformative Exercises

- Encourage your son to talk to family, friends, or community members about their experiences and thoughts. It's an excellent way for him to improve at listening and valuing ideas.

- Set a goal to perform a certain number of random acts of kindness each week. It could be anything like lending a hand to someone living next door, giving to charity, or just throwing someone a kind word.

- Create a scenario involving a conflict or misunderstanding and take turns pretending to be each person involved. It's a solid way to get the hang of stepping into someone else's shoes and smoothing things when they get sticky.

- Discuss current events or social issues with your son, encouraging him to ask questions, look at things from different angles, and start shaping his own well-thought-out takes.

- Reading books together gives you a window into being kind, compassionate, and standing up for what's right. Talk about what the folks in the stories go through and how they relate to real-world issues.

Chapter 8: Building Resilience: Bouncing Back from Challenges

"It is not the strongest of the species that survives, nor the most intelligent that survives. It is the one that is most adaptable to change." - Charles Darwin

Life is a journey filled with highs and lows. It's like trekking a winding trail with surprises around every corner, throwing challenges that test our limits and push us to grow. Resilience is about tackling them directly, absorbing the lessons they teach, and coming out tougher than before.

Think of resilience as a stronger muscle with each hurdle you leap over. It's the ability to adapt, persevere, and find the strength within ourselves to keep moving forward even when the going gets rough. For young guys, developing resilience is akin to donning a suit of armor, readying them for life's inevitable knocks, and giving them the enthusiasm to step out into the world with boldness and bravery.

One of the components of building resilience is fostering a growth mindset. This concept, brought into the spotlight by psychologist Carol Dweck, revolves around the idea that our abilities and intelligence can be honed through dedication, learning, and persistence.

When boys adopt a growth mindset, they view challenges as chances to stretch their capabilities. They recognize that bumps in the road aren't defeats but milestones on the journey to achievement. They trust in their capacity to learn, adapt, and tackle barriers, even when adversity strikes.

Parents play a crucial role in instilling a growth mindset in their boys. Rather than praising intelligence or talent, it's all about applauding the hard work, perseverance, and strategies for improving. Urge them to take on challenges, to see slip-ups as chances to learn, and to stay the course toward their ambitions.

Here's how you can encourage a growth mindset:

- **Emphasize the power of "yet":** If your boy faces a challenge, inspire him to add "yet" to his statements. Rather than "I can't do this," he can say, "I can't do this yet." This minor tweak in wording bolsters the belief that he can learn and improve with effort.

- **Celebrate effort and progress:** Celebrate his efforts, even if instant success isn't on the cards. Focus on the strides he's making, the abilities he's honing, and the insights he's gaining.

- **Lead by example with a growth mindset:** Demonstrate to your boy that you, too, embrace challenges and see mistakes as chances to grow. Share your stories of learning and overcoming hurdles, showing that resilience is a journey that lasts a lifetime.

Equipping boys with problem-solving skills is another vital piece of the resilience puzzle. When a problem arises, they need the know-how to pinpoint the issue, brainstorm fixes, and take steps to conquer it.

Teaching problem-solving can be broken down into bite-sized chunks:

- **Identify the problem:** Assist your boy in defining the challenge at hand. What's the nitty-gritty of the problem? What obstacles need to be tackled?

- **Brainstorm solutions:** Push him to develop various potential solutions, no matter how outlandish they may initially seem. The aim is to spark creativity and consider multiple options.

- **Weigh the solutions:** Guide him in evaluating the pros and cons of each potential fix. Which are doable? Which are likely to hit the mark?

- **Pick a solution and act:** Encourage him to select a fix and spring into action. Be his cheerleader as he executes his plan, offering support and motivation.

- **Reflect on the outcome:** After he's put his solution to the test, help him think about the results. Was it successful? What lessons can be gleaned? How might he adjust his approach in the future?

By teaching problem-solving skills, you empower your son to take control when facing challenges and to devise solutions. You foster a sense of agency and self-belief, building his confidence in his ability to overcome obstacles and achieve his goals.

Learning from experiences, both positive and negative, is another crucial aspect of building resilience. Encourage your son to reflect on his experiences, to pinpoint the lessons learned, and to apply those lessons to future hurdles.

When he encounters a setback, guide him to see it as a chance to grow. Pose questions like, "What have you learned from this?" or "How can this experience shape your growth?" This approach helps him develop a growth mindset and fortify his resilience for what lies ahead.

Fostering resilience is not about creating invincible boys impervious to life's rough patches. It's about arming them with the mindset and tools to maneuver through life's ebbs and flows with assurance, bravery, and a steadfast belief in their power to surmount obstacles and realize their dreams.

Developing a Growth Mindset in Boys

Imagine a young boy learning how to ride a bicycle. He's shaky, takes a tumble, and has bruised knees. But each time he falls, he hops right back on, tweaks his approach, and gives it another shot. He doesn't think of his tumbles as setbacks; instead, he sees them as chances to get better. That is what we call a growth mindset—this idea that our skills aren't set in stone but can be built up with some elbow grease, sticking with it, and learning from the oops moments.

We're handing them a superpower when we nurture this kind of mindset in boys. We tell them they can conquer any challenge and unlock their true potential. It's all about getting them to believe that they're not stuck where they are skill-wise; they can always level up with some hard work and grit.

Boys with a growth mindset don't look at tough times as something to dread. Nope, they get a kick out of them, seeing each one as a fantastic chance to grow and stretch their limits. They get that slip-ups aren't the end of the world but are helpful feedback to help them tweak their game plan. They face roadblocks with a "bring it on" vibe, sure that they've got what it takes to get past them and hit their targets.

This mindset is about believing in the magic of putting in the effort, learning from the whoopsies, and having the guts to keep at it, even when the going gets rough.

Developing a growth mindset is like planting a tiny seed that will eventually bloom. It needs some love, a bunch of cheers, and a steady stream of support. If we cheer on their hard work, make a big deal out of every little win, and show them how it's done by living that growth mindset, we can help our boys build up this super belief in what they can do.

With a growth mindset, boys aren't just ready to face challenges; they're pumped to take them head-on, learn a ton, and become more demanding and competent. They turn into forever students, always looking for the next hurdle to jump over and confident that what they can achieve is limitless.

Equipping Boys with Problem-Solving Skills

Picture this: Your kid has a massive barrier in his way. Teaching him how to solve problems is similar to handing him a set of gadgets to climb over, dig beneath, or perhaps even find a way around it. It's all about giving him the strength to face challenges as intriguing riddles waiting to be cracked.

Problem-solving is an essential life skill that stretches past schoolwork or specific jobs. It's an attitude, a particular way of tackling problems with an active, can-do perspective. When boys get good at figuring things out, they build up this cool self-belief in their power to get past hurdles and reach their dreams.

Let's break it down:

- **Spot the problem:** What's the big issue here? Get him to spell out the hurdle he's up against and chop it into tinier bits that are easier to handle.

- **Think up solutions:** Toss around a bunch of different fixes, even the wild or wacky ones. This stirs up creative thinking and opens up possibilities.

- **Weigh your options:** Look at each possible fix's good and bad sides. Which ones make the most sense? Which ones have the best shot at working? Help him think about what might happen with each choice.

- **Make a move:** Pick a fix and go for it. This part requires courage and taking initiative because it's about stepping into new territory and taking a gamble.

- **Look back and learn:** Once the fix is in play, think it over. Did things pan out? How could it get better? What did you learn? This part is great for learning and growing from every single try.

Getting the hang of this method teaches boys to hit challenges with a sense of control and cleverness. They get ready to face problems, knowing they've got what it takes to find solutions and achieve their goals.

This method is about building critical thinking skills, inventiveness, and grit. It's about prepping boys to be dynamic problem-solvers who can handle twists and turns with assurance and guts.

Key Points

- Resilience is a Muscle: Resilience is a skill that can be built and strengthened with deliberate effort and practice.

- Growth Mindset Boosts Resilience: Instilling the belief in boys that their skills can improve with hard work and learning is crucial for nurturing their resilience.

- Praise Effort, Not Just Outcomes: Focus on praising effort, perseverance, and strategies for improvement rather than just focusing on achievements or talents.

- Problem-Solving is a Superpower: Equipping boys with problem-solving skills gives them the tools to tackle challenges, find solutions, and reinforce their confidence in conquering hurdles.

- Experience is the Best Teacher: Encourage boys to reflect on all their encounters, the good and the bad, to extract valuable insights and use those takeaways for future challenges.

Self-Reflection Questions

1. How would you describe your mindset? Are you more inclined towards a growth perspective, or do you lean towards a fixed viewpoint? And do you think your thoughts are shaping your son's attitude?

_____

_____

_____

_____

_____

2. When your son faces a challenge or setback, how do you react? Do you offer encouragement and support, or do you unintentionally discourage him?

_____

_____

_____

_____

_____

3. When it comes to celebrating your son's achievements and efforts, where's your focus? Are you cheering on the learning journey, the hustle, or the final win?

_____

_____

_____

_____

_____

4. Does your boy get the hang of tackling problems? Is he good at spotting issues, coming up with solutions, and getting into gear to sort things out?

_____

_____

_____

_____

_____

5. What steps can you take to ensure your home is where your son can toughen up? How can you give him chances to take on tough stuff, make mistakes, and become more assertive on the other side?

_____

_____

_____

_____

_____

Transformative Exercises

- Jot down many challenges on pieces of paper and place them in a jar. Take turns pulling out a slip and then, as a team, devise ways to tackle the problem.

- When your son experiences a setback, help him see it as constructive feedback. Discuss what he can learn from the experience and how he can use that knowledge moving forward.

- Create a list of positive affirmations that reinforce a can-do attitude, such as "I can learn anything," "Mistakes help me grow," or "I get tougher with every challenge."

- Throw some "what-if" scenarios at your son with different challenges and encourage him to put on his thinking cap and map out what he'd do.

- Create a visual display to celebrate your son's efforts and progress, even if he doesn't succeed immediately. Whether it's a bulletin board, a whiteboard, or a simple notebook, it's all about celebrating the journey.

Chapter 9: Raising Boys to be Respectful and Responsible

"Respect your efforts, respect yourself. Self-respect leads to self-discipline. When you have both firmly under your belt, that's real power." - Clint Eastwood

Nurturing boys to be respectful and responsible is about developing a solid inner sense of right and wrong—a moral compass that steers their behaviors and dealings with the world around them. It's about helping them understand that their decisions impact themselves and others.

At the heart of respect is the act of valuing oneself and others. It means acknowledging every person's inherent value and dignity, regardless of age, background, or beliefs. When boys learn to respect themselves, they're more inclined to show respect to others, establish healthy boundaries, and advocate for their convictions.

To teach self-respect, we've got to walk the talk. As parents, we should demonstrate self-value by looking after our physical and emotional health and standing firm in our beliefs and needs. We should also respect our sons by considering their views, affirming their emotions, and appreciating their uniqueness.

Respecting others means guiding boys to be kind, courteous, and thoughtful. It's about teaching them to listen well, respectfully communicate, and handle disagreements without hostility. It also encourages them to value diversity, welcome differences, and stand against bias and injustice.

Healthy boundaries are crucial for respect. They outline what's acceptable in behavior for us and others. Teaching boys to set these boundaries involves helping them feel okay about saying "no" when something doesn't sit right with them, expressing their needs and likes, and safeguarding their physical and emotional health.

Conflict resolution skills are crucial for working through disagreements and finding peaceful solutions. Teach your son to listen intently, share his views calmly and respectfully, and look for good outcomes for everyone. Help him view conflict not as a fight to win but as a chance to understand and grow.

Respectful communication is the cornerstone of solid relationships. It's about choosing kind words, listening well, and speaking clearly and respectfully. Teach your son to avoid name-calling, insults, and other verbal aggression. Encourage him to assertively share his feelings and needs while considering others' viewpoints.

Responsibility and accountability are intertwined with respect. When boys realize their actions have repercussions, they're more likely to make thoughtful choices and own up to their slip-ups.

Setting clear expectations is crucial for promoting responsibility. Be upfront about your expectations for behavior, chores, schoolwork, and other duties. Consistently apply consequences for good and bad behaviors, helping him see the connection between his actions and the results.

Giving boys chances to make decisions lets them take charge of their lives. Let him make choices suited to his age, like picking his clothes, choosing activities, or deciding how to spend leisure time.

This builds a sense of independence and accountability for his decisions.

Encouraging him to take responsibility means helping him understand that he's in charge of his choices. When he messes up, encourage him to admit it, say sorry if needed, and learn from it. Avoid blaming or shaming; focus on fostering a sense of accountability instead.

Raising boys to be respectful and responsible is a continuous journey that demands patience, consistency, and dedication to exemplify these virtues ourselves. It's about cultivating a family culture of respect, where everyone feels valued, listened to, and responsible for their deeds. By instilling these values in your son, you're not just shaping his character but enabling him to become a constructive and active member of society.

Instilling Respect for Self and Others

Respect is a two-way street, a constant give-and-take of value between a person and those around them. Teaching respect to boys lays down a strong foundation for their character, which supports healthy relationships, ethical decision-making, and a sense of accountability for their actions.

Self-respect is the cornerstone. It means acknowledging his value, embracing his strengths, and overcoming his flaws. When a boy holds himself in high regard, he's less prone to accept being disrespected, more likely to establish clear boundaries, and tends to make decisions that reflect his principles.

This self-respect grows from unconditional love and acceptance. It's encouraged by recognizing his emotions, respecting his viewpoints, and honoring his uniqueness. It's reinforced when he sees you exemplifying self-respect in your daily life.

Respecting others naturally follows from self-respect. It involves treating everyone with warmth, politeness, and thoughtfulness, regardless of age, background, or creed. It's about understanding that everyone deserves to be treated with dignity.

This respect is shown in day-to-day deeds: listening intently, speaking gently, lending a hand, and resolving conflicts peacefully. It's about valuing diversity, embracing differences, and standing against bias.

Teaching respect isn't about setting strict rules or insisting on obedience. It's about understanding that everyone is worthy of respect and kindness. It's about cultivating a home environment where compassion, knowledge, and responsibility are cherished most.

Promoting Responsibility and Accountability

Imagine a young boy planting a seed in the garden. He waters it diligently, ensures it gets enough sunlight, and patiently waits for the first signs of life. Fostering a sense of responsibility and accountability in him is much like caring for that seedling, offering the necessary support and direction to help it transform into a strong and flourishing plant.

Taking responsibility means owning up to our actions and promises. It involves recognizing that our decisions lead to outcomes, and we must bear the consequences, affecting us and others.

Being accountable is about embracing responsibility for everything we do, good or bad. It means admitting when we err, learning from these slip-ups, and, where needed, making things right.

To instill these values in boys, start by setting clear guidelines. Communicate what you expect of them regarding behavior, chores, schoolwork, and other duties. Ensure he knows what you anticipate from him and the repercussions for either meeting or failing to meet these standards.

Give him chances to make choices. Letting him decide on his outfit, which activities to engage in, or how to use his leisure time can help him feel in control and answerable for his life choices.

If he stumbles, steer him toward recognizing his mistakes without casting shame or pointing fingers. Teach him about the ripple effect of his actions and motivate him to set things right if needed. This approach imparts valuable lessons about accountability and instills a sense of responsibility for his decisions.

Consistency is crucial. Enforce consequences like rewards or penalties, both positive and negative. This helps him understand the link between his actions and their outcomes, reinforcing his understanding of responsibility.

Promoting responsibility and accountability empowers them to become responsible young men. It's about nurturing their growth, guiding their development, and supporting them as they grow into individuals who can positively impact society.

Key Points

- **Self-Respect is Essential:** To respect others, one must start with self-respect. This means recognizing your needs, establishing clear boundaries, and respecting one's beliefs.

- **Showing Respect Takes Many Forms:** When you respect someone, it's about being kind and polite, paying attention when they speak, communicating in a considerate way, valuing different cultures, and standing against bias.

- **Setting Boundaries is Crucial:** Young men must learn to set appropriate boundaries. This teaches them to know their rights, express their needs, and protect their mental and physical health.

- **Learning to Handle Disagreements:** It's beneficial to teach boys how to resolve conflicts by listening actively, negotiating, and aiming for solutions that everyone can agree on.

- **Owning Your Actions Matters:** Encouraging boys to be responsible involves setting clear rules, letting them make choices, and helping them understand the importance of taking responsibility for what they do.

Self-Reflection Questions

1. How do you demonstrate self-respect in your everyday activities? Are you mindful of your health? Do you establish firm limits and communicate your needs clearly and confidently?

_____

_____

_____

_____

_____

2. In what ways do you guide your son to show respect to others? Do you highlight the importance of being kind, showing empathy, and striving to understand when interacting with him and those around him?

_____

_____

_____

_____

_____

3. How comfortable is your son setting boundaries and saying "no" when something doesn't sit right

with him? What steps can you take to help him improve this critical life skill?

_____

_____

_____

_____

_____

4. When disagreements arise within your family, how do you go about addressing them? Do you lead by example, showing how to engage in respectful discussions and solve problems together?

_____

_____

_____

_____

_____

5. What strategies do you use to foster a sense of responsibility and accountability in your son? Do you lay out clear rules, give him chances to make choices, and back him up as he learns to take responsibility for his actions?

_____

_____

_____

_____

_____

Transformative Exercises

- Try out different scenarios involving disagreements or conflicts and role-play how to communicate respectfully, using "I" statements and active listening.

- Discuss situations where setting boundaries might be necessary and devise ways to do that without stepping on toes.

- Gather the family for a meeting to discuss what's expected regarding behavior, household duties, and other obligations. Ensure your son has a say in creating these guidelines and understands the potential outcomes of not following them.

- Give your son chances to make choices suitable for his age, like picking out his outfit, deciding on fun activities, or handling a bit of pocket money.

- When your son makes a mistake, help him learn to own up to it, say sorry when needed, and figure out how to make things right. This allows him to learn to be responsible and accountable for his actions.

Chapter 10: Navigating Friendships and Social Connections

"A single rose can be my garden... a single friend, my world." -
Leo Buscaglia

Friendships are a crucial part of a young boy's life. It's where he finds his tribe, learns who he is, and gets that all-important sense of support. As he grows up, friendships get more layered, shaping his beliefs, actions, and self-image.

Helping these friendships flourish is about guiding boys thoughtfully and helping them grow the tools for solid, respectful, and understanding relationships.

Talking things out is the heartbeat of any good friendship. Encourage your kid to share what's on his mind and to be honest with his friends. Show him how to hear someone out, value different viewpoints, and speak up about his needs and limits.

Compromise is another essential ingredient in successful friendships. Teach your boy that it's OK to balance his wants with those of his friends. Push him to aim for solutions that make everyone happy, building a sense of fairness and teamwork.

Knowing where to draw the line is super essential for keeping friendships healthy. Make sure your son knows it's OK to say "no" if he's not down with something, to lay out his comfort zone, and to look after himself. Teach him to respect others' boundaries, creating a two-way street of respect.

Social dynamics can be complex, especially in the teen years. Boys might face being left out, caving to peer pressure, or dealing with bullies. These moments can be tricky, making them feel alone, hurt, and lost.

If your son feels left out, be there for him. Let him talk it out, encourage him to find his squad, and dive into his passions and talents.

Peer pressure is about teaching your son to stand his ground and hold on to his values. If things get heavy, remind him that he's got adults in his corner.

Bullying is a big no-no. It can mess with a kid's head and heart. If your son is facing this, jump into action. Hear him out, give him your full support, and team up with the school or other adults to stop it.

Helping boys navigate these challenges requires building vital social skills, such as:

- **Initiating conversations**: Teach your son how to break the ice and find things in common with others.

- **Active listening:** Encourage him to listen well, ask questions, and care about what friends say.

- **Getting how others feel:** Help him step into someone else's shoes to build empathy and kindness.

- **Cooperation and compromise:** Stress the importance of working together and developing solutions that benefit everyone involved.

- **Assertiveness:** Urge him to express his needs and opinions confidently and respectfully while valuing others' views.

Building these skills is a process. Give your boy chances to mingle in different settings, like hangouts, sports, or community events. Encourage him to try new stuff, meet new faces, and stretch his boundaries.

Supporting Healthy Peer Relationships

Think of good friendships among peers as like a blossoming garden. As parents, we're the caretakers, creating a rich soil and a warm environment for these bonds to grow strong.

To support these healthy friendships, begin by encouraging open conversations. Get your son to share his experiences with his friends, the good and bad times. Listen with an open mind, ready to guide and support when necessary.

It's crucial to teach him to pick his friends thoughtfully. Urge him to connect with those who align with his values, respect his boundaries, and cheer on his development. Help him spot the signs of solid friendships, like trust, faithfulness, and mutual respect.

Social skills are the toolkit for nurturing friendships. Show your son how to initiate conversations, listen intently, and express his needs and emotions clearly. Teach him empathy, to see things from another's viewpoint, and to handle disagreements calmly.

Setting boundaries is like putting a fence around that garden, keeping the bad stuff out. Teach your son it's perfectly fine to say "no" when something doesn't feel right, communicate his limits, and look after his health. Encourage him to respect others' boundaries, building a culture of shared respect and understanding.

We must do the same for our sons' friendships as gardeners would water and shine light on their plants. Encourage him to hang out with his mates, participate in activities they enjoy, and create happy memories together.

Addressing Social Challenges and Bullying

Imagine a playground with children, each learning the ropes of social interactions. Some kids make friends with ease, while others grapple with fitting in and dealing with issues like being left out, succumbing to peer influence, or facing bullies.

These social hurdles are akin to challenges on the playground that test a child's adaptability and interpersonal abilities. Being excluded can be as lonely as sitting on the sidelines, watching others play. Peer pressure might push him toward actions that clash with his principles, tempting him to engage in behaviors that compromise his values.

Bullying is like a bully blocking the slide, using their power to intimidate, harm, or exclude others. It comes in various forms, from physical aggression to verbal taunts or even subtle social exclusion.

Addressing these challenges calls for a proactive and supportive approach. If your son is dealing with exclusion, guide him to find new groups or hobbies where he can bond with like-minded peers. Help him to embrace and hone his unique abilities, fostering confidence and a strong sense of self.

In the face of peer pressure, teaching him to spot the signs and craft ways to stand by his beliefs is crucial—practice scenarios with him, showing how to decline gracefully yet firmly. Point out reliable adults he can turn to for support when facing peer pressure.

Bullying demands a decisive and swift reaction. Hear out your son with compassion and acknowledge his emotions. Equip him with the skills to assert himself when it's right. School staff or other authorities should be involved in tackling the issue and ensuring his safety if needed.

Key Points

- **Friendships are Essential:** For boys, friendship provides a sense of belonging, support, and opportunities for honing social skills and exploring their identity.

- **Communication Matters:** The bedrock of solid friendships is effective communication, which includes attentive listening and clearly articulating one's needs.

- **Finding Middle Ground Enhances Peace:** It's important to teach boys the value of compromise and the art of seeking mutually beneficial outcomes to strengthen their connections with others.

- **Healthy Limits Foster Mutual Respect:** Teaching boys to establish and honor personal boundaries is crucial, ensuring their friendships remain respectful and well-balanced.

- **Social Challenges are Opportunities for Growth:** Encountering issues like feeling left out, succumbing to peer influence, or dealing with bullies is part of growing up, but with the proper support and skill-building, boys can emerge stronger from these situations.

Self-Reflection Questions

1. How would you describe your son's friendships? Does a network of dependable friends surround him, or does he find making connections challenging?

_____

_____

_____

_____

_____

2. How do you assist your son with the intricacies of social interactions? Do you share advice on communicating effectively, finding a middle ground, and establishing personal boundaries?

_____

_____

_____

_____

_____

3. How does your son cope when faced with feelings of being left out or the pressures that come from his peers? Is he equipped with the

self-assurance and tools necessary to stand up for his beliefs and requirements?

_____

_____

_____

_____

_____

4. What steps does your family take to tackle the issue of bullying? Do you discuss it openly and arm your son with tactics to deal with such situations?

_____

_____

_____

_____

_____

5. What strategies could you employ to enhance your son's social abilities and help him forge solid and positive friendships?

_____

_____

_____

_____

_____

Transformative Exercises

- Discuss the qualities that make someone a good friend and create a list of essential values in friendships, such as trust, respect, honesty, and kindness.

- Cook up different communication scenarios on slips of paper (e.g., expressing a need, disagreeing respectfully, setting a boundary) and take turns acting them out.

- Create a scenario involving a conflict between friends and role-play different ways to resolve the conflict peacefully and respectfully.

- Discuss different types of peer pressure and come up with some slick moves for standing your ground, all while keeping it honest with what you believe in.

- Engage in activities raising awareness about bullying, such as reading books, watching videos, or participating in community events. Discuss different forms of bullying and strategies for responding to it effectively.

Chapter 11: The Role of Fathers and Male Role Models

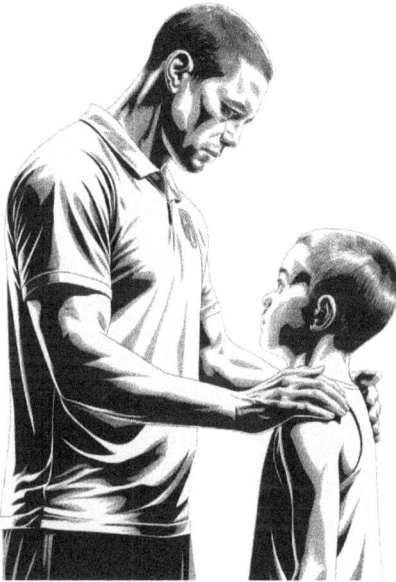

"When a father gives to his son, both laugh; when a son gives to his father, both cries." - William Shakespeare

A dad's influence on his son's life is immense, shaping who he becomes, his beliefs, and how he perceives the world. This connection is built on moments spent together, quiet words of wisdom, and a mutual, unspoken understanding. Fathers and any positive male figures are essential in guiding a young boy's emotional growth, offering direction, support, and a real-life example of manhood.

Studies have repeatedly shown that boys with engaged dads are more likely to manage their emotions well, interact better socially, and have a stronger sense of self-worth. They're less prone to taking dangerous risks and more likely to excel in school. A father's love and direction lay a strong foundation for a boy to explore his feelings, carve out his identity, and tackle life's hurdles.

Being an involved dad isn't just about being there physically—it's also about connecting emotionally. It's about forging a relationship with your son that goes beyond meeting his basic needs and tapping into his emotional core.

Here are a few ways dads can bond with their sons on an emotional level:

- **Spend quality time together:** Do things together that you both enjoy, like sports, DIY projects, hiking, or just chatting. These moments build memories and strengthen your relationship.

- **Show you care:** Give hugs, offer encouragement, and perform little acts of kindness. Let your son know you're proud and have faith in him.

- **Be a good listener:** When your son talks, put everything aside, look him in the eye, and hear him out. Acknowledge his emotions, provide support, and assure him you're always there.

- **Share your stories:** Talk about your life, the ups and downs, and the lessons you've learned. Being open about your vulnerabilities can encourage him to share his own.

- **Be a role model:** Show your son what it means to be a good man by demonstrating respect, responsibility, empathy, and integrity in your own life.

- **Lead by example:** Demonstrate what it means to be a decent man by living with respect, responsibility, empathy, and honesty.

Dads have a unique opportunity to show their sons how to express emotions healthily. By sharing your feelings honestly and freely, you teach your son that it's normal to experience everything from joy and excitement to sadness and fear.

Have deep talks about feelings. Discuss your feelings, why you feel them, and how you deal with them. Urge your son to do the same, fostering a space for candid and open talks about emotions.

Another crucial part of being a dad is offering guidance and support. Be there for your son when facing challenges, offering encouragement, advice, and a listening ear. Help him develop problem-solving skills, build resilience, and confidently navigate life's complexities.

Fathers, along with all positive male models, deeply influence a boy's emotional growth. By being present, involved, and supportive, you help your son grow into a confident, tough, and emotionally savvy man. You equip him with the skills to handle life's obstacles, forge strong bonds, and realize his tremendous potential.

The Importance of Positive Male Influence

Think of a young boy as a sapling reaching for the sun. The good men in his life are akin to solid props that help him grow straight and strong, offering steadiness, direction, and a blueprint to achieve his utmost capacity. These figures could be dads, uncles, grandpas, mentors, or coaches—any man who exemplifies admirable traits and principles.

So, why do these figures matter so much? Boys pick up a lot by watching and copying the actions of those they look up to and hold in high esteem. **Having good male role models is like having a live demo of what it takes to be a stand-up guy, highlighting attributes such as:**

- **Emotional intelligence:** Sharing feelings correctly, understanding and caring for others, and forging solid bonds.

- **Responsibility and accountability:** Owning up to what you do, sticking to your word, and being someone, others can count on.

- **Respect and integrity:** Treating others with kindness and consideration, fighting for the good stuff, and being truthful and just.

- **Resilience and perseverance:** Getting past tough spots, bouncing back after a fall, and pursuing goals with determination.

These role models don't just show off good qualities; they're there to provide guidance and support. They offer a listening ear, a shoulder to lean on, and a cheer when you need it. They're the ones helping boys get through rough patches, grow their confidence, and carve out a strong personal identity.

Good male role models are also crucial in molding a boy's view of what it means to be manly. They toss out the old, confining ideas of manhood and prove that being tough and tender aren't mutually exclusive. They teach boys that it's okay to let your guard down, show your feelings, and reach out for a helping hand when it gets tough.

In a world where boys are often bombarded with conflicting messages about what being a man is, these positive male figures are like a trusty guide, leading them towards a wholesome and rewarding concept of manhood. They help shape boys into confident, caring, and accountable grown-ups, ready to do good in their communities and beyond.

Engaging Fathers in Emotional Development

Picture this: a dad and his boy building a tower together, brick by brick. Now, think of a father's role in his son's emotional growth as an extra layer to that structure. It's not just about adding height; it's about reinforcing it, making it tough, and enhancing its beauty.

Fathers have a unique and powerful influence on their sons' emotional lives. Their presence, guidance, and example mold how boys perceive and manage their feelings. When dads dive into their sons' emotional upbringing, they forge a connection more profound than mere words, a link that goes beyond words, a connection that fosters emotional intelligence, resilience, and a sense of belonging.

It all begins with being there fully—present in body and spirit. It's about resonating with your son's emotions, hearing him with all your heart, and meeting him with compassion and insight. It's about crafting an environment where he's at ease to share his highs, his lows, and his soft spots.

Showing your son the ropes of handling emotions is like giving him the blueprint for his emotional journey. By sharing your feelings genuinely and without filters, you show him that it's perfectly normal to experience a spectrum of emotions, from excitement and joy to sadness and anger.

Deep talks about feelings are like cementing those bricks together, solidifying your connection. Share your emotions, why you're feeling that way, and how you cope with those emotions. Encourage your son to do the same, creating a dialogue that builds understanding and connection.

Offering guidance and support is akin to building scaffolding around a tower, providing a steady and safe structure as your son grows and learns. Stand by him during tough times with encouragement, advice, and a listening ear. Help him develop problem-solving skills, build resilience, and confidently navigate life's complexities.

Bringing fathers into emotional development is not about turning them into therapists but equipping them to be the emotional cornerstones their sons rely on. It's about nurturing a bond that encourages emotional intelligence, toughness, and a sense of inclusion, laying down a solid base for a future filled with sound relationships and emotional health.

Key Points

- **Fathers are Essential for Emotional Growth:** Dads are vital in nurturing their boys' emotional smarts, self-worth, and ability to interact with others. Their active role gives boys a solid foundation of safety and acceptance, encouraging them to explore their emotions and develop healthy coping mechanisms.

- **Being There Emotionally Counts:** When dads tune in, show compassion, and offer a judgment-free zone, it gives boys the courage to share their inner world.

- **Leading by Example Speaks Volumes:** When fathers demonstrate that it's perfectly fine to experience and share a broad spectrum of emotions, they're equipping their sons with the tools for emotional literacy and self-awareness.

- **Meaningful Conversations Strengthen Bonds:** When fathers and sons have genuine, open talks about feelings, it brings them closer and paves the way for valuable life lessons and support.

- **Guidance and Support Foster Growth:** Dads who guide and back up their boys are setting them up to tackle life's

hurdles, bounce back from setbacks, and
confidently step into the world.

Self-Reflection Questions

1. Can you describe your relationship with your
father or other male role models? How have your
experiences with them, both good and bad,
influenced your views on what it means to be a
man and how to handle emotions?

_____

_____

_____

_____

_____

2. What ways do you find to bond emotionally with
your boy? Are you carving out time for activities
and heart-to-hearts that bring you closer and show
him affection?

_____

_____

_____

_____

_____

3. Are you at ease when it comes to showing your feelings, especially around your kid? Do you demonstrate how to deal with emotions healthily, or do you tend to suppress your feelings?

_____

_____

_____

_____

_____

4. When your son is angry or sad, how do you respond? Do you offer support and guidance, or are you downplaying or ignoring his emotional state?

_____

_____

_____

_____

_____

5. How can you become more actively involved in your son's emotional development? What steps can you take to strengthen your connection and ensure he gets emotional support?

_____

_____

_____

_____

_____

Transformative Exercises

- Set up a consistent weekly catch-up conversation with your son to share your feelings and experiences from the past week.

- Schedule dedicated time each week to do something fun together that you love, whether it's hitting a ball around, tackling a creative project, or taking a stroll.

- Fill a container with open-ended questions like "What are you grateful for?" or "What are you most proud of?"

- Make a conscious effort to express your feelings openly and genuinely when you're with your son, to show him how it's done.

- Start a shared journal where you and your son can write letters to each other, sharing your thoughts, feelings, and experiences. It's a great way to strengthen your bond and keep the lines of communication wide open.

Conclusion

As we reach the end of this journey together, let's take a moment to look back on the path we've traveled. We've explored the intricate landscape of boys' emotional lives, revealed the hidden challenges they face, and discovered the power of intentional parenting in shaping their emotional well-being.

We've come to understand that boys, often constrained by a limiting "boy code," might find it hard to share their feelings, leading to suppressed feelings, communication struggles, and unhealthy ways of dealing with stress. Yet, we've also discovered that emotional intelligence is not a fixed trait but a skill that can be nurtured and strengthened through intentional parenting.

Reflect on the key insights we've collected:

- **Understanding the Inner World of Boys:** We've seen how crucial it is to grasp the difficulties boys grapple with, questioning the restrictive norms that hinder them from expressing their emotions and providing a haven for their true selves to shine.

- **Building a Foundation of Connection:** We've emphasized the significance of being there, actively listening, and showing empathy to forge solid bonds with our children that encourage open dialogue and trust.

- **Navigating Anger:** We've investigated the origins of boys' anger, sharing methods for calming, self-control, and positive expression, thus equipping them to handle anger constructively.

- **Taming Anxiety:** We've learned to spot anxiety symptoms in boys and introduced relaxation techniques, mindfulness, and thinking strategies to soothe their inner turmoil and strengthen their resilience.

- **Confronting Sadness and Depression:** We've broken down the stigma surrounding depression in boys, providing guidance on spotting the signs and supporting those dealing with grief and depression.

- **Fostering Self-Awareness and Emotional Literacy:** We've stressed the need to assist boys in recognizing and naming their emotions, broadening their emotional language, and expressing their feelings in healthy, both spoken and unspoken, ways.

- **Cultivating Empathy:** We've looked at how empathy develops in boys and shared ways to foster this vital trait through understanding others' perspectives, acts of kindness, and deep conversations about societal issues.

- **Building Resilience:** We've discovered strategies for nurturing a can-do attitude in boys, providing them with problem-solving tools and ways to overcome obstacles, helping them recover from challenges and emerge stronger.

- **Raising Boys to be Respectful and Responsible:** We've discussed the importance of instilling self-respect and respect for others, teaching boundaries and conflict resolution, and promoting responsibility and accountability.

- **Navigating Friendships and Social Connections:** We've given tips on nurturing healthy friendships, tackling social issues like exclusion and peer pressure, and developing robust social skills for complex social interactions.

- *The Role of Fathers and Male Role Models:* We've illuminated the pivotal role dads and male figures play in boys' emotional growth, urging them to be actively involved by setting an example of healthy emotional sharing, engaging in meaningful talks, and offering support.

These insights aren't just theoretical; they're practical tools for a hopeful future for our boys, shaping their emotional health, relationships, and success.

As parents, we are deeply responsible for guiding and cultivating the upcoming generation of men. Intentional parenting isn't about perfection or having all the answers; it's about consistently showing up for our sons with affection, understanding, and a readiness to learn and evolve with them.

It's about fostering a home where feelings are acknowledged, shared, and comprehended. It's about teaching our sons to accept their emotional selves, share their feelings genuinely, and navigate life's complexities with resilience and compassion.

Raising boys isn't always straightforward. We'll face obstacles, setbacks, and moments of uncertainty. But remember, you're not in this alone. Seek out support from fellow parents, mentors, or professionals when necessary. Trust your gut, lean on your love for your son, and never lose faith in him.

The rewards of intentional parenting are immeasurable. When we raise emotionally savvy boys, we're not just molding individuals but crafting a better future for everyone. We're creating a world where empathy, understanding, and connection flourish. We're bringing up men who are strong and successful but also caring and compassionate and capable of forming meaningful bonds and contributing positively to society.

So, as you continue raising your son with intention, bear in mind the significant influence you wield in his life. Embrace the hurdles, rejoice in the victories, and never underestimate the power of your love and guidance. You are molding the future, one boy at a time.

This book is merely the starting point. It's a guide, a source of encouragement, and a reminder of your extraordinary influence as a parent. But the real adventure unfolds in your daily moments with your son—in your talks, your laughter, your tears, and your shared life experiences.

Cherish those times, treasure them, and never cease to learn and grow with your son. The future is promising, and with your purposeful guidance, your son can flourish in every aspect of his life.

THANK YOU

Dear Reader,

Thank you for joining me on this journey. I hope that the insights, strategies, and stories shared in these pages have resonated with you and provided you with valuable tools to empower your son on his path to becoming an emotionally resilient and compassionate young man.

As a token of appreciation, I'd like to offer you a gift for you and your son. Just scan the QR code below to access the file.

If this book has touched your heart or made a difference in your family's life, I would like you to consider leaving a review. Your feedback is invaluable and helps other parents discover this guide and embark on their own journey.

Thank you again. I wish you all the best on your parenting adventure!

With warm regards,
Myron Wingen.

SCAN ME

Printed in the USA
CPSIA information can be obtained
at www.ICGtesting.com
CBHW051614111224
18825CB00030B/1008